Descent into Nightmare

By the Editors of Time-Life Books

Alexandria, Virginia

TIME
LIFE ®

Time-Life Books is a division of
Time Life Inc., a wholly owned subsidiary of

**The Time Inc. Book Company
Time-Life Books**

PRESIDENT: Mary N. Davis

Managing Editor: Thomas H. Flaherty
Director of Editorial Resources:
Elise D. Ritter-Clough
Director of Photography and Research:
John Conrad Weiser
Editorial Board: Dale M. Brown, Roberta Conlan,
Laura Foreman, Lee Hassig, Jim Hicks, Blaine
Marshall, Rita Thievon Mullin, Henry Woodhead
*Assistant Director of Editorial Resources/Training
Manager:* Norma E. Shaw

PUBLISHER: Robert H. Smith

Associate Publisher: Ann M. Mirabito
Editorial Director: Russell B. Adams, Jr.
Marketing Director: Anne C. Everhart
Production Manager: Prudence G. Harris
Supervisor of Quality Control: James King

Editorial Operations
Production: Celia Beattie
Library: Louise D. Forstall
Computer Composition: Deborah G. Tait
(Manager), Monika D. Thayer,
Janet Barnes Syring, Lillian Daniels
Interactive Media Specialist: Patti H. Cass

The Cover: A frightened fifteen-year-old member of
a Luftwaffe antiaircraft crew bursts into tears after
being taken prisoner by the Americans near Gies-
sen in west-central Germany in the spring of 1945.
Bled dry of able-bodied men, Adolf Hitler turned in
desperation to Germany's children, using them at
first in civil defense roles but eventually plunging
tens of thousands of teenage boys into combat. The
youngsters were armed only with obsolete weapons, rudimentary training, and heavy doses of Nazi
propaganda.

The Third Reich

SERIES EDITOR (Acting): John Newton
Series Administrator: Philip Brandt George
Editorial Staff for *Descent into Nightmare:*
Senior Art Director: Raymond Ripper
Picture Editor: Jane Jordan
Text Editors: Paul Mathless, Henry Woodhead
Senior Writer: Stephanie A. Lewis
Associate Editors/Research: Katya Sharpe Cooke,
Oobie Gleysteen, Trudy Pearson
Assistant Art Director: Lorraine D. Rivard
Senior Copy Coordinator: Ann Lee Bruen
Picture Coordinator: Jennifer Iker
Editorial Assistant: Alan Schager

Special Contributors: Ronald H. Bailey,
Charles Clark, Donald Dale Jackson (text);
Martha Lee Beckington, Barbara Fleming, Linda
Lee, Anthony J. Sheehan, Marilyn Murphy Terrell
(research); Roy Nanovic (index)

Correspondents: Elisabeth Kraemer-Singh
(Bonn), Christine Hinze (London), Christina
Lieberman (New York), Maria Vincenza Aloisi
(Paris), Ann Natanson (Rome). Valuable
assistance was also provided by: Glenn Mack,
Juan Sosa (Moscow), Elizabeth Brown, Katheryn
White (New York), Traudl Lessing (Vienna).

First printing. Printed in U.S.A.

Published simultaneously in Canada.
School and library distribution by Silver Burdett
Company, Morristown, New Jersey 07960.

TIME-LIFE is a trademark of Time Warner Inc.
U.S.A.

**Library of Congress Cataloging in
Publication Data**
Descent into nightmare / by the editors of
Time-Life Books.
    p.   cm. — (The Third Reich)
    Includes bibliographical references and index.
    ISBN 0-8094-7037-3
    ISBN 0-8094-7038-1 (lib. bdg.)
    1. World War, 1939-1945—Campaigns.
2. Germany-History—1933-1945. I. Time-Life
Books. II. Series.
D743.D383 1992   91-28936
940.54'1—dc20   CIP

For information on and a full description of any
of the Time-Life Books series listed above, please
call 1-800-621-7026 or write:
Reader Information
Time-Life Customer Service
P.O. Box C-32068
Richmond, Virginia 23261-2068

General Consultants

Col. John R. Elting, USA (Ret.), former associate professor at West Point, has written
or edited some twenty books, including
*Swords around a Throne, The Superstrate-
gists,* and *American Army Life,* as well as
Battles for Scandinavia in the Time-Life
Books World War II series. He was chief con-
sultant to the Time-Life series The Civil War.

Charles V. P. von Luttichau is an associate
at the U.S. Army Center of Military History in
Washington, D.C., and coauthor of *Command Decision* and *Great Battles.* From 1937
to 1945, he served in the German air force
and taught at the Air Force Academy in Berlin. After the war, he emigrated to the United
States and was a historian in the Office of the
Chief of Military History, Department of the
Army, from 1951 to 1986, when he retired.

Contents

Luftwaffe ground personnel salute a careworn Adolf Hitler in the fall of 1944 during one of his last visits to a forward air base. Walking beside Hitler is his devoted pilot, Hans Baur, who began flying for the aspiring Führer in 1932 during the whirlwind election campaigns that brought Hitler and the Nazi party to national prominence.

A Desperate Effort to Hold the West

The letter from Field Marshal Günther Hans von Kluge found its way to Adolf Hitler's desk the end of August 1944. "When you receive these lines, I shall be no more," wrote the recently deposed commander in chief West, who had served as one of Hitler's senior generals since the invasion of Poland in 1939. "Life has no more meaning for me. I cannot bear the accusation that I sealed the fate of the West by taking wrong measures. I am dispatching myself where thousands of my comrades have already gone."

After outlining the reasons why he had failed to stop the Allied drive across France and expressing doubt that his successor could do better, Kluge made an anguished plea: "Should the new weapons in which you place so much hope, especially those of the Luftwaffe, not bring success, then, my Führer, make up your mind to end the war. The German people have suffered so unspeakably that it is time to bring the horror to a close. There must be ways to obtain this objective and above all to prevent the Reich from falling under the Bolshevist heel. I have steadfastly stood in awe of your greatness, your bearing in this gigantic struggle, and your iron will. If fate is stronger than your will and your genius, that is destiny. You have made an honorable and tremendous fight. History will testify this for you. Show now that greatness which will be necessary if it comes to the point of ending a struggle that has become hopeless."

The Führer read the letter in silence, then handed it to his loyal aide General Alfred Jodl, chief of operations of the armed forces high command (OKW). Hitler abruptly canceled the state funeral he had planned and saw to it that the cover story for Kluge's death—a cerebral hemorrhage—was superseded by quiet word that the disgraced field marshal had in fact swallowed potassium cyanide.

Several days afterward, Hitler met with Generals Siegfried Westphal and Hans Krebs before their departure to the collapsing western front. Kluge, Hitler confided, had been under investigation as a traitor and "might have been arrested immediately had he not taken his own life." "I don't want this to leak out," he told them disingenuously, because it "would foster contempt for the army."

A Luftwaffe infantryman gives directions to the crew of a 116th Panzer Division half-track, camouflaged with pine boughs, during Germany's surprise counteroffensive through the Ardennes Forest in December 1944. The six-week battle earned the Reich a brief breathing spell, but it consumed irreplaceable reserves of men and matériel.

7

A month earlier, on July 20, an attempt had been made to assassinate the Führer at a war conference held at the guest barracks of his eastern front headquarters in East Prussia. A number of army officers were involved, and Hitler claimed he had evidence linking Kluge to them. (In fact, several of the conspirators had served on Kluge's staff on the eastern front, although Kluge himself had never been an active participant in the plot.) The Führer was determined that he never again would be let down by his generals.

Hitler related his baseless suspicions that Kluge had intended to negotiate a truce with the British and Americans. Talk of ending the struggle, he assured the two generals, was out of the question. "At a time of heavy military defeats," he explained, "it is quite childish and naive to hope for a politically favorable moment to make a move. The time will come when the tension between the Allies becomes so strong that, in spite of everything, the rupture occurs. History teaches that all coalitions break up, but you must await the moment, however difficult the waiting may be. I intend to continue fighting until there is a possibility of a decent peace. Whatever happens, we shall carry on this struggle until, as Frederick the Great said, 'One of our damned enemies gives up in despair!' "

The man Hitler had chosen to rescue the western front—Field Marshal Walther Model—was untouched by the wave of suspicion sweeping over the officer corps. The fifty-four-year-old commander sported a trademark monocle and liked to refer to himself as the "Führer's fireman"—with good reason. During the past nine months of fighting against the Soviets, Hitler had put him temporarily in charge of three different army groups after sacking their commanding officers. Each time, Model restored the German lines, prompting Hitler to call him the "savior" of the eastern front—even though Model sometimes accomplished his defensive feats in defiance of Hitler's own no-withdrawal orders. In January 1942, when Model's Ninth Army had been in danger of being cut off by the Russians near Rzhev, he had dared to gainsay Hitler to his face, asking him, "Who commands the Ninth Army, my Führer, you or I?" Yet he had been one of the first generals to affirm his loyalty after the July assassination attempt. Model was in Berlin to receive the prestigious diamond clasp for his Knight's Cross of the Iron Cross on August 17 when the Führer impetuously appointed him to replace the hapless Kluge.

Model arrived at Kluge's western theater headquarters at La Roche-Guyon that same night to face his biggest challenge yet. Both of the German army groups in France were in grave danger. Two days earlier, the Allies had made their long-anticipated second landing in southern France, and General Johannes Blaskowitz's overmatched Army Group G, assigned the

Squeezing the Reich from Two Directions

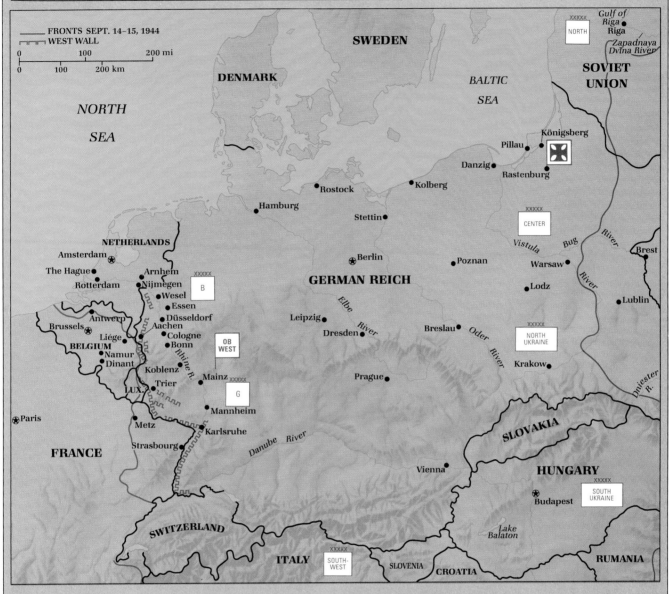

During the summer of 1944, the German army suffered a series of crushing defeats that drove it back toward the borders of the Reich on both the eastern and the western fronts. In the east, the German forces struggled to recover from the Red Army's virtual annihilation of Army Group Center in Belorussia and retreated across the Vistula River into central Poland. In the meantime, the German armies in the Baltics lost Riga and were pushed onto the Courland peninsula. In August, the Russians launched a new offensive in the Balkans that overran Rumania, captured the oil fields at Ploesti, and carried the fight into Bulgaria, Yugoslavia, and Hungary. After breaking out of their Normandy beachheads, the Anglo-American forces were able to advance rapidly, liberating Paris on August 25 and moving into Belgium and the Netherlands. On September 4, the British captured Antwerp; eight days later, the Franco-American invasion force that had landed on the French Mediterranean coast in August linked up with the other Allied armies north of Dijon. By mid-September, the Allies had reached the West Wall, Hitler's prewar border fortifications, where the German defense lines finally stabilized.

impossible task of defending the entire French Mediterranean coast, was in full retreat northward along the Swiss border.

Army Group B faced more imminent peril. Leaderless since July when Field Marshal Erwin Rommel was wounded in a British strafing attack, its Seventh and Fifth Panzer armies were trapped in Normandy by an Allied encirclement at Falaise. Although Army Group B's other force, the Fifteenth Army, was still intact, it was pinned against the English Channel coastline in its Atlantic Wall fortifications. The previous spring, Hitler had earmarked the Fifteenth Army as the Wehrmacht's primary anti-invasion force and had deployed it along the Pas-de-Calais, where he insisted that the Allies would make their primary landing. Now the Fifteenth Army was in danger of being cut off and taken from the rear. In addition to his theater responsibilities, Model, like Kluge before him, also took direct command of the fragmented Army Group B.

Although the Germans had been in France and the Low Countries for more than four years, Hitler had refused to consider constructing interior defensive lines in case the Atlantic Wall failed to deter an invasion. Nothing had become of an OKW plan to build a belt of fortifications across France, along the Somme, the Marne, and the Saône rivers. Thus, when Model extricated the remnants of the Fifth Panzer Army and Seventh Army from the Falaise pocket and brought them back across the Seine, the Germans did not pause until they reached defensible positions along the Meuse and the tributaries of the Rhine in Belgium and Holland. The Fifteenth Army, meanwhile, withdrew along the coast to another major northern European water barrier, the Scheldt. In the meantime, to the south, Army Group G pulled back to the Vosges Mountains near Alsace.

Since the Normandy landings, the western command had lost about 300,000 men; an additional 200,000 were penned up in isolated coastal fortresses behind the Allied lines. Model estimated that his entire force of seventy-four divisions, spread thinly across the 480-mile-long front from the North Sea to the Swiss border, represented the equivalent of no more than twenty-five normal divisions. There were fewer than 100 serviceable tanks in the entire theater.

Still, Hitler vowed to turn the tables, boasting he would "Dunkirk" the Allies and again drive them from the Continent. He intended to block the Allied advance at the West Wall, the band of fortifications built in 1938 to protect Germany's western border, and wait for winter weather. "Fog, night, and snow," he said, would offer a "great opportunity."

The Allies, meanwhile, pressed their pursuit. By the end of August, thirty divisions were either at or across the Seine River. General Sir Bernard Law

Montgomery's Twenty-first Army Group, consisting of the First Canadian Army and the British Second Army, had reached the Somme River in northern France and prepared to advance into Belgium. To the south was Lieut. General Omar N. Bradley's U.S. Twelfth Army Group. Its U.S. First Army was spread between the Oise and Meuse rivers, aiming for Mons and Namur in a direct path to Aachen, the traditional western gateway to Germany, and its U.S. Third Army was on the upper Meuse River, heading for Metz and Nancy. Farther south, Lieut. General Jacob L. Devers's Sixth Army Group, a Franco-American force consisting of the U.S. Seventh Army and the French First Army, lined up in front of the southern reaches of the Vosges Mountains and prepared to advance into Alsace.

The Allies had reached positions they had not expected to achieve until the spring of 1945, and they were unsure of how to exploit their astonishing success. Though optimistic that he could end the war quickly, General Dwight D. Eisenhower, commander in chief of the Allied forces, faced a difficult strategic choice—whether to continue the attack on a broad front, as had been the original pre-D-day plan, or, as Montgomery now advocated, to allow the Twenty-first Army Group to make a single thrust of immense power through Belgium and Holland, cross the Rhine River, and encircle the Ruhr, Germany's vital industrial region.

The looming question facing Eisenhower was how to resupply the advancing armies when the Allies had the use of only a single port, Cherbourg in Normandy, 350 miles behind the front. Until the port of Antwerp could be captured and put into service, shortages—particularly of fuel—would make it impossible for all of the Allied armies to remain on the attack. For Montgomery's plan to work, the lion's share of incoming supplies would have to be funneled to him.

Although British and American planners had sincere military differences on how best to end the war, the issue was further complicated by the fact that Montgomery, a British general, had been in command of all Allied ground forces since D-day. For the Anglo-American alliance, questions of grand strategy could rarely be separated from personalities and politics. In the summer of 1944, the numbers in the field spoke for themselves: American soldiers outnumbered British soldiers by three to one. Given that fact, public opinion in the United States would never sanction a continuation of the present command structure. In addition, many of the top American generals believed that Montgomery's towering ego was the driving force behind his strategic arguments, which seemed designed to subordinate Bradley and shut off the fuel supply to the aggressive, fast-moving U.S. Third Army of Lieut. General George S. Patton. Under pressure from the Roosevelt administration and army chief of staff, General George C. Marshall, to have an American commander in the field, Eisenhower opted to assume the position himself, effective September 1, 1944.

Meanwhile, Montgomery slammed into the Germans with a ferocity neither Hitler nor Model could have imagined. The armies of the British Twenty-first Army Group leaped forward seventy-five miles from the Somme River and took Brussels, the Belgian capital, on September 3. The following day, the German garrison in Antwerp abandoned the city. In their quick retreat northward, the Germans failed to destroy the docks and electric sluice gates, leaving the port facilities virtually undamaged.

The Allies, however, could not benefit from the port. Although Montgomery's drive into Belgium had isolated the Fifteenth Army of General Gustav von Zangen in a coastal pocket west of Antwerp, Zangen's troops controlled the West Scheldt estuary, a fifty-mile-long waterway that was the port's lone shipping channel to the sea. The Scheldt, heavily mined and with German guns lining both banks, would have to be cleared before the Allies could use Antwerp.

Montgomery's quick thrust into Belgium led to desperate calls to Model from the German high command urging him to "Hold! Hold! Hold!" On the day Antwerp fell, Model reported to Hitler that for Army Group B to maintain its line along the Scheldt, the Albert Canal, the Meuse River, and the West Wall, he needed twenty-five fresh divisions with an armored reserve of five to six panzer divisions. Otherwise, Model warned, the "gateway into northwest Germany will be open."

It was an impossible request. The only fresh divisions ready for combat had been sent to General Blaskowitz's Army Group G in August to help block the advance of Patton's U.S. Third Army toward the upper Moselle River in eastern France.

Germany was already scraping the bottom of its manpower barrel. SS chief Heinrich Himmler, the new head of the Reserve Army, had raised forty new *Volksgrenadier* (People's Infantry) divisions. Drawn in large measure from Hitler Youth and other Nazi party sources, these troops were for the most part not yet ready for combat. The army, in the meantime, was drafting men as old as fifty, pressing clerks, drivers, cooks, and other rear-echelon troops into front-line duty, and folding into the ranks Luftwaffe airmen and Navy sailors who had been idled by the lack of fuel for their planes and ships. The Germans were even forming units of convalescents pulled from the military hospitals.

Thus Hitler had little to offer—until Reich Marshal Hermann Göring stepped forward. The Luftwaffe chief had 20,000 paratroopers either in training or recuperating from past actions. Combining them with the troops in Holland and another 10,000 Luftwaffe ground personnel, Göring had enough men to provide what would become the First Paratroop Army. To lead this new army, Hitler selected General Kurt Student, a veteran of the 1940 airborne assault against Rotterdam and of the 1941 paratroop invasion of Crete. On Hitler's orders, Student and his army departed for Belgium to deploy along the Albert Canal.

The speed of the Allied advance forced Model to shift his headquarters almost daily to avoid being captured. Constantly on the move, he was largely out of touch with Army Group G and spending all of his time running Army Group B. Not a man to mince words, Model's repeated complaints and abrasive demands for reinforcements won him no friends at OKW headquarters. In just two weeks time, he had lost his effectiveness as commander in chief West.

A German soldier climbs through an opening in the bars of a lion cage at the Antwerp Zoo to join fellow prisoners of war, including a Kriegsmarine sailor *(dark uniform).* **The Allies converted the zoo into a holding pen for POWs and Belgian collaborators after the fall of Antwerp on September 4, 1944.**

On September 5, Hitler replaced Model with Field Marshal Gerd von Rundstedt, who had served as the western theater commander before Kluge. A veteran of the 1940 campaign in France and the 1941 invasion of the Soviet Union, the trusted, old-guard Prussian officer was seen as a delegator and a prop for the falling morale of the officer corps. Even Model welcomed Rundstedt's appointment because it allowed the combative general to focus his considerable energy on rallying Army Group B.

As Model had warned, the Allies quickly established bridgeheads over the Albert Canal and the Meuse River and closed in on the West Wall. Rundstedt, newly installed in his headquarters at Ziegenberg near Koblenz, reported to Hitler that it would take six weeks to adequately strengthen the West Wall defenses. The chain of 3,000 concrete bunkers and pillboxes, stretching from Germany's border with Holland in the northwest to its border with Switzerland in the southwest, had been modernized in 1940. After four years of neglect, however, the wall had become overgrown with trees, underbrush, and wildflowers. Much of its barbed wire, mines, and communications equipment had been stripped for use in the Atlantic Wall. The fortifications had fallen into such disuse that its caretakers had trouble finding keys to the emplacements.

By September 8, the Americans had captured the city of Liége in eastern Belgium. Enjoying complete freedom of movement, they began probing attacks along the West Wall's outer belt near Aachen. For the first time in the war, the ground fighting had reached German soil. Henceforth, Hitler instructed Rundstedt, "every foot of ground, not merely the fortifications, is to be treated as a fortress."

Suddenly, after the long retreat from France, the German armies miraculously recovered their balance. Taking full advantage of having interior supply lines, Model established a lengthy new line of defense along the West Wall. Morale was also lifted by the arrival of the highly respected General Hasso-Eccard von Manteuffel from the eastern front. Manteuffel took command of the Fifth Panzer Army, now a part of Blaskowitz's Army Group G, and immediately began making plans for a counterattack against Patton in eastern France.

For the Allies, the second week of September marked a major shift in strategy. Using gangs of conscripted laborers, the Germans were working feverishly to strengthen the West Wall, and it was rapidly becoming a forbidding obstacle. Moreover, Allied fuel and ammunition supplies had literally run out. At a meeting on September 10 in Brussels, Eisenhower and his top commanders weighed Montgomery's single-thrust proposal. The usually cautious British general, recently promoted to the rank of field marshal, now proposed one of the most daring operations of the war. He

Attempting to make the West Wall defensible again, conscripted Reich Labor Service workers dig an antitank ditch near the Dutch border in late summer 1944. One German general described the condition of the long-neglected belt of fortifications as "pitiable."

suggested using Allied airborne troops, now in reserve, to make a landing deep behind German lines, along the Neder Rijn River (Lower Rhine) in Holland. The bold thrust would allow the British Twenty-first Army Group to outflank the West Wall in its most northerly position and cut off the German Fifteenth Army in western Holland. If the plan succeeded, Montgomery would be in perfect position to encircle the Ruhr.

Eisenhower approved the two-part plan, code-named Operation Market-Garden. The Market portion would be the largest airborne operation of the war and the first for the Allies in daylight. Some 20,000 paratroopers and glider-borne infantry would land near the Dutch towns of Eindhoven, Nijmegen, and Arnhem. Over a four-day period, they would capture and hold several bridges spanning the three major rivers: the Maas (Meuse), the Waal (Rhine), and the Neder Rijn, as well as several canals, until a linkup could be effected with ground forces advancing from sixty miles away in the Garden portion of the plan. Market's most important objective—and the one requiring the deepest penetration of German-held territory—would be the highway bridge over the Neder Rijn at Arnhem.

Garden would be carried out by the XXX Corps of General Sir Miles C. Dempsey's British Second Army. The XXX Corps, made up of two infantry divisions and a tank brigade, would power its way up a corridor to Arnhem all the way to the Zuider Zee. For XXX Corps to be successful, the Allied paratroopers had to seize control of the two-lane, fifty-mile-long highway that ran from Eindhoven to Nijmegen and on to Arnhem.

Operation Market-Garden was highly risky, relying as it did on several consecutive days of good flying weather and on weak opposition. The airborne troops would have to take and hold their objectives without the

benefit of heavy weapons—and depend on the ground force and its 20,000 vehicles to make a rapid advance along a single narrow highway.

Hitler and the German high command were well aware that the Allies had yet to deploy their airborne forces. Expecting some kind of operation west of the Rhine, Field Marshal Model, on September 11, received intelligence reports that the Allies were assembling landing craft in British ports across the English Channel. Model assumed that an invasion of the Netherlands was in the works. As late as the morning of September 17, notices of "conspicuously active" Allied sea and air reconnaissance off the Dutch coast fostered his apprehension that a sea and air landing was about to take place in northern Holland.

Model alerted his forces in the region: the Armed Forces Netherlands guarding the coastal region, and elements of the II SS Panzer Corps that happened to be refitting in the Arnhem area. He also transferred the 59th Infantry Division from the Fifteenth Army to Student's First Paratroop Army, which, by chance, was located near Eindhoven in transit to southeastern Holland. But neither Model nor any other German commander had any idea of the scope of the airborne operation they were about to face.

At one o'clock in the afternoon on Sunday, September 17, following a thunderous Allied bombing attack, 1,545 transport planes and 478 gliders carrying 20,000 men of the U.S. 82d and 101st and British 1st Airborne divisions appeared in the skies. Escorted by nearly 700 fighters, the huge air armada met only token resistance from the Luftwaffe, although German antiaircraft guns brought down several planes. By 2:30 p.m., almost all of the British and American paratroopers had landed safely.

At his headquarters at Vught, nine miles west of one of the American drop zones, Student heard what he later described as a "roaring in the air of such mounting intensity that I left my study and went onto the balcony. Wherever I looked," he said, "I saw aircraft, troop carriers, and large aircraft towing gliders. An immense stream passed low over the house. I was greatly impressed, but during these minutes I did not think of the danger of the situation." To his chief of staff, he remarked, "Oh, how I wish I had had such powerful means at my disposal!"

Dutch villagers rushed out to shower the landing troops with flowers and food, but soon hurried back into their homes when the Germans opened fire. Model's headquarters in the Arnhem suburb of Oosterbeek west of the city happened to be in the middle of the British drop zone. Hastily packing his belongings, Model moved to the headquarters of II SS Panzer Corps, located eighteen miles east of Arnhem, where he took personal control of the battle and called for reinforcements.

Shortly after the assault began, the Germans had an incredible stroke of

An SS man searches the grounds of a Dutch estate on the Lower Rhine west of Arnhem, where a British paratrooper's chute hangs snagged on a nearby building. The paratrooper was part of a massive Allied airdrop that began Operation Market-Garden on September 17, 1944.

good fortune. German antiaircraft gunners shot down one of the American gliders. When ground troops examined the enemy dead, they discovered a complete copy of the Allied operational orders. By three o'clock in the afternoon, the orders were on Student's desk. Henceforth, the Germans knew every move the Allies would attempt.

Two of three British 1st Airborne battalions that had landed at Oosterbeek were stopped by heavy fire from the 9th SS Panzer Division. The third battalion, however, managed to reach Arnhem and capture the northern end of the vital Neder Rijn highway bridge—the key to the success of the whole operation. But the Germans at the southern end refused to be budged. Over the next few days, heavy fog and rain prevented the British from landing reinforcements. As elements of the 9th SS Panzer Division whittled down the British bridgehead, the 10th SS Panzer Division and a force made up of units of the Armed Forces Netherlands hammered away at the tenacious paratroopers.

The 101st Airborne fared somewhat better. After landing at Eindhoven and fanning out quickly, the Americans captured four of their five assigned bridges with little difficulty. The task force attempting to take the Wilhelmina Canal bridge north of Eindhoven encountered stiff resistance from 88-mm guns. The time it took for the Americans to destroy the German guns was just enough to allow the Germans to blow the bridge. It went up in smoke as the Americans arrived. Crossing the canal on a pontoon bridge, the Americans settled down to wait for XXX Corps.

SS men watch a shell explode near a German armored vehicle on a street in Oosterbeek. They were part of a force organized by Field Marshal Walther Model to prevent the British 1st Airborne Division from reaching Arnhem and seizing the vital Neder Rijn highway bridge.

At Nijmegen, the 82d Airborne came under heavy fire from the 9th SS Panzer Division's Reconnaissance Battalion and fell behind schedule. Although the Americans seized the bridge at Grave and captured the high ground near Nijmegen, by the time they reached the large highway bridge, the Germans had formed a solid defense.

Led by tanks of the Irish Guards, the XXX Corps began its drive toward Eindhoven on the afternoon of September 17. Racing north, the Irish Guards collided with Task Force Walther, a patchwork German unit consisting of two paratroop battalions, two SS battalions, and a penal battalion. The Germans destroyed eight tanks before they were overcome by British infantry supported by fighter-bombers.

Late the next day and thirty hours behind schedule, XXX Corps linked up with the 101st Airborne in Eindhoven. After British and American engineers replaced the blown bridge over the Wilhelmina Canal, the British

A dead German soldier lies on the bridge over the Waal River at Nijmegen. Troops from the U.S. 82d Airborne Division and the British Grenadier Guards Regiment seized the 600-yard-long span on September 20, 1944.

pushed on toward Nijmegen, along the road the Americans dubbed "Hell's Highway." The fighting continued for nine days. The XXX Corps tried its utmost to reach the trapped paratroopers, but Student's First Paratroop Army, firing from orchards and farmyards along the highway, stopped the British force three miles short of Arnhem.

On September 25, Montgomery called off the attack. The Allies had gouged a sixty-mile-deep salient into Holland, but failed to outflank the West Wall and the Rhine. In addition, the Germans had inflicted more than 13,000 casualties at a cost of only 3,300 losses of their own.

Throughout the late summer and early fall, the Germans continued to build up their battered forces. Scouring the country for new sources of manpower, the government once again broadened eligibility for conscription. Himmler's Volksgrenadiers now swept up boys as young as sixteen. School vacations were extended indefinitely so that children aged twelve and older could be sent into factories or antiaircraft units. Young women sixteen to twenty-five now had to register for war duties.

Propaganda minister Joseph Goebbels had already announced a new civilian mobilization program that mandated a sixty-hour workweek. Armaments minister Albert Speer reported to Hitler that although Allied bombing had damaged the oil and ammunition industries, war production had actually increased. Thanks to Speer's improvisations, an average of 1,500 tanks and self-propelled assault guns and 9,000 vehicles were rolling off the production lines each month. The vital ball-bearing industry was also largely intact, despite several major attacks by Allied bombers. And the output of new fighter planes reached its highest level of the war.

The impressive numbers of armaments, however, did not always translate into strength in battle. When Manteuffel's Fifth Panzer Army launched a counterattack against Patton at Lunéville, the two attacking panzer brigades included tanks fresh from the factory. Their crews were equally new, and after several days of fighting, the Americans won a resounding victory. One routed brigade was reduced from ninety-eight panzers to seven. Many of the German losses were due to simple mechanical failures. The debacle forced Manteuffel to abandon the French provincial capital of Nancy.

Angered over Army Group G's inability to counter Patton, Hitler dismissed Blaskowitz and installed in his place General Hermann Balck, a veteran of the eastern front. "Your task, General Balck," Hitler informed him, "will be to get by with the fewest possible troops. Under no circumstances can troops be diverted to you."

Established at his headquarters near Strasbourg, Balck ordered Manteuffel to resume his attack on September 25, this time with the Fifth Panzer

A captured British paratrooper gestures defiantly at the German photographer who snapped this picture of him and his mates being marched to the Arnhem railroad station for shipment to Germany. He was one of 6,000 British soldiers seized by the Germans in and around Arnhem.

Army's armored reserves as well. With Allied air support grounded by bad weather, Manteuffel got off to a good start. But then the skies cleared, and Allied planes pounded Manteuffel's forces. On September 29, Hitler reluctantly called off the attack. He ordered all available armor shifted to the north to protect the Ruhr.

At the beginning of October, the Allies launched their first full-scale assault on the West Wall around Aachen. The ancient city, birthplace of

Charlemagne and seat of his medieval empire, was an important symbol to the German people and to the Nazi party, which viewed Charlemagne as the precursor of the Holy Roman Empire, or First Reich. Aachen was already a bombed-out ruin, and most of its population had been evacuated, but its capture was critical to the Allies' strategy for crossing the Rhine.

For Aachen's defense, General Friederich J. M. Köchling, commander of the Seventh Army's LXXXI Corps, mustered a nominal four divisions. He deployed the 183d Volksgrenadier and 49th Infantry divisions north of the city; the 246th Volksgrenadier Division inside the city limits; and the 12th Infantry Division on the southeastern outskirts. The force totaled no more than 18,000 men, backed up by 239 pieces of artillery.

Lieut. General Courtney H. Hodges's U.S. First Army would begin its attack from the north. An infantry division followed by armored units of the XIX Corps would move across the Würm River, a small, north-south stream running east of the city and guarding the so-called Aachen Gap, the ancient gateway to the open country of the Cologne plain. This force would join the VII Corps infantry, which would breach the West Wall from the south.

After several postponements and some softening up of the German defenses by American fighter-bombers, Major General Leland S. Hobbs's 30th Infantry Division spearheaded the attack on October 2. The Americans achieved a degree of surprise, as the Germans were distracted by diversionary attacks near Geilenkirchen, ten miles to the north. After fighting off several counterattacks, the Americans rooted out the dug-in defenders with dynamite charges and flamethrowers. By October 6, they had established a bridgehead over the Würm.

Field Marshal Model, accompanied by the Seventh Army commander, General Erich Brandenberger, arrived at the LXXXI Corps command too late to organize a counterattack. Reporting to Rundstedt, Model stated that the "situation around Aachen has grown more critical. Unless replacements arrive, continued reverses will be unavoidable."

After relaying Model's message to OKW on October 10, Rundstedt sent in four reserve panzer divisions. The reinforcements began arriving the same day, but because the Germans were so desperate, Model decided to send the panzer units into the battle piecemeal. The same day, the Americans issued an ultimatum calling for the German forces in Aachen to surrender unconditionally within twenty-four hours or face further bombardment. Lieut. Colonel Maximilian Leyherr, a regimental commander in the 246th Volksgrenadier Division who was in temporary charge of the garrison, rejected the demand.

Following an intense air attack, the Americans advanced on the city. On October 12, Colonel Gerhard Wilck, the commander of Leyherr's division,

Troops from the U.S. 9th Infantry Division pass through "dragon's teeth" antitank barriers south of Aachen on September 13, 1944. In the next three months, stiffening German resistance and American supply problems kept penetrations to a dozen miles.

arrived to take over Aachen's defense. After receiving infantry reinforcements, he mounted two counterattacks that prevented the Americans from closing their circle around the city until October 16. Rundstedt ordered Wilck to "hold this venerable German city to the last man, and, if necessary, allow himself to be buried under its ruins." Over the next few days, Wilck exhorted his troops to "fight to the last man, the last bullet in fulfillment of our oath to the flag. Long live the Führer!"

Despite the fiery words, Wilck capitulated on October 21 along with 11,000 of his soldiers. "When the Americans start using 155s as sniper weapons," he remarked wryly, "it is time to give up." The first German city had fallen. But victory had cost the U.S. First Army nearly 6,000 casualties. Hodges had used up almost all of his artillery ammunition and was in no condition to continue the offensive. Here and elsewhere along the front, the problem of supplies once again interfered with the Allied campaign, and the crux of the problem was Antwerp.

By the beginning of October, the Allies had held Antwerp for nearly a month but did not have use of its port because the West Scheldt estuary remained in German hands. Between September 6 and 22, General Zangen extricated 86,000 troops and 6,000 vehicles of the Fifteenth Army from the south bank of the Scheldt where they had been driven by Montgomery's advance. While most of the divisions continued the retreat northward into Holland and Germany, Hitler ordered Zangen to leave behind three divisions to protect the Scheldt. Zangen anchored his defenses on Walcheren Island. As one of the original Atlantic Wall strongpoints, it was a formidable obstacle, bristling with powerful coastal batteries and concrete bunkers.

Walcheren Island and the South Beveland peninsula, connected by a narrow causeway, formed the north bank of the estuary. Zangen assigned the 70th Infantry Division to defend Walcheren, while deploying the 245th Infantry Division on South Beveland. He left the 64th Infantry Division on the estuary's south bank, basing them in the port town of Breskens where the Scheldt joins the North Sea. Ten miles to the south, the Leopold Canal, running roughly parallel to the Dutch-Belgian border, blocked the landward approach to Breskens, aiding the German defense.

With Market-Garden over, and the hoped-for quick strike across the Rhine and into the Ruhr no longer possible, the Allies needed to open up the port of Antwerp more urgently than ever. Montgomery assigned the task of clearing the Scheldt to the II Canadian Corps, with assistance from the Royal Air Force (RAF) and several thousand Commandos.

On October 2, the Canadian 2d Division brushed aside light German resistance in the Belgian countryside north of Antwerp and advanced ten

The First Defeat on Home Soil

On October 19, 1944, Colonel Gerhard Wilck, commander of the 246th Volksgrenadier Division defending Aachen, realized that his chances of preventing the first German city from falling into Allied hands were diminishing by the hour. As the coronation site of thirty-two emperors and kings of the Holy Roman Empire, Aachen was an important symbol of national socialism's purported link with Germany's distant past. Now it was encircled by the U.S. VII and XIX corps, and the Americans were moving in for the kill.

As American riflemen penetrated the rubble-strewn streets, systematically blowing up building after building, Wilck exhorted his troops: "The defenders of Aachen will prepare for their last battle. We shall fight to the last man." But two days later, when the Americans wheeled a 155-mm self-propelled rifle directly in front of a large bunker in the center of the city—the headquarters of Wilck himself—the colonel ignored his own melodramatic exhortation.

After two German soldiers were killed while trying to communicate Wilck's willingness to capitulate, the German commander solicited help from the American prisoners that he was holding inside the headquarters bunker. Two of them volunteered. When they dashed out into the street waving a white flag, the firing ceased, and by nightfall, the city of Aachen was completely under American control.

Colonel Wilck (*far right*), Aachen's commander, reviews a map of the area with Field Marshal Model.

Racing to a defensive position in an Aachen churchyard, a Volksgrenadier with a Panzerfaust antitank weapon passes a line of *Sturmgeschütz* III assault guns.

Squeezed between a Sherman
tank and a stone wall, an
American soldier fires down a
street in Aachen. The ancient
city's defenders lacked the
firepower to compete with the
American armor and artillery.

A German reconnaissance
officer briefs his men on the
outskirts of Aachen. When the
fighting stopped, an American
observer declared the city "dead
as a Roman ruin"—but miraculously unscathed was Aachen's
cathedral, which contained the
royal tomb of Charlemagne.

miles to the town of Woensdrecht, strategically located just inside the Dutch border at the intersection of the South Beveland causeway and the mainland. There, the Canadians met stiff opposition from Task Force Chill, a mixed group of veteran and inexperienced soldiers led by Lieut. General Kurt Chill. The task force included the remnants of three infantry divisions, portions of the Hermann Göring Replacement Training Regiment, and the tough 6th Paratroop Regiment. Originally sent to the area to help stop Operation Market-Garden, Task Force Chill kept the Canadians at bay for two weeks before finally retreating north on the Dutch mainland, opening the causeway to South Beveland.

While the fight for Woensdrecht went on, the RAF began a series of bombing raids against Walcheren Island. On October 3, an attack by 247 Lancaster bombers breached the major dike of the island. The North Sea surged across the middle of the saucer-shaped island, herding the Germans and the Dutch civilians onto the high ground of three narrow coastal strips, including Walcheren's two main towns, Flushing and Middelburg, on opposite coasts of the island. Driven into their strongpoints, the Germans remained as formidable as ever.

On the southern bank of the Scheldt, the Canadian 3d Division attacked Major General Kurt Eberding's 64th Infantry Division. Advancing behind flamethrower tanks, the Canadians established two bridgeheads across the Leopold Canal, bottling up the Germans in a position that became known as the Breskens pocket. Exhorted by Eberding, the Germans dug in. The general warned the troops that surrender would be regarded as desertion and "in cases where the names of individuals are ascertained, these will

Guarding the seaward approach to Antwerp at the mouth of the West Scheldt estuary, Walcheren Island bristles with German weaponry. The torpedo launcher at left, aimed by a member of the naval coastal artillery, was part of a network of powerful coastal batteries overlooking the North Sea. Elsewhere on the island fortress, German soldiers man machine-gun nests camouflaged with netting *(right)*. The 8,000-member garrison lived in bomb-proof, concrete bunkers that were dug into the dunes *(below)*.

be made known to the civilian population at home, and their next of kin will be looked upon as enemies of the German people."

The coastal batteries on Walcheren Island, firing across the estuary, helped Eberding hold off the Canadians until October 21, when RAF Typhoon bombers knocked them out. That same day, the Canadians broke through into Breskens. But pockets of stubborn Germans held out until November 3—one day after Eberding himself gave up.

Meanwhile, the fight for the South Beveland peninsula had begun between the Canadian 2d Division and the German 245th Division. Aided by amphibious assaults across the Scheldt, the Canadians finally won control of the peninsula on October 26. The remnants of the German forces withdrew to Walcheren Island to join forces with the 70th Division, bringing the German troop strength under Lieut. General Wilhelm Daser to 10,000. Although Breskens and South Beveland had fallen, the German stranglehold on the Scheldt continued because Walcheren Island—the most formidable obstacle—remained in their hands.

Before dawn on November 1, the Canadians attacked across the narrow causeway connecting the South Beveland peninsula with Walcheren Island and established a temporary bridgehead. Distracted by the incursion, the Germans were late to react to the primary attack, an amphibious landing by British, French, and Dutch commandos at Flushing, where the German batteries had been severely crippled by the Typhoons during the October 21 air strike. As the commandos advanced into the town, twenty-five landing craft armed with rockets and light artillery attacked Walcheren's western coast. The German coastal guns sank nine landing craft and damaged eleven more. But under cover of the artillery exchange, another group of commandos landed. By nightfall, the commandos had overrun the two main batteries on the western side of the island.

The Germans on the southern coast of Walcheren Island continued to fight. On November 4, yet another Allied commando force came ashore behind them. Cut off and running out of ammunition, the Germans realized that further resistance was futile. On November 6, a lieutenant of the Royal Scots Regiment met with General Daser in Middelburg. Daser was ready to surrender, but not to a lowly lieutenant. Awarding himself a "local and temporary" promotion to lieutenant colonel, the young officer now had sufficient standing to satisfy the general, and the surrender was executed. At last, the estuary was under Allied control.

The tenacious German stand had succeeded in delaying Allied use of the port of Antwerp for an additional precious month, however, and had resulted in 13,000 Allied casualties. And because the Scheldt still had to be swept of mines, the first Allied supply ship would not be able to tie up at

The icy North Sea surges over Walcheren Island on October 4, 1944, one day after British bombers smashed the 300-foot-wide Westkapelle dike, one of the oldest and sturdiest in Holland. Despite the flooding, the German troops on the island held out for another month.

the docks until November 28—nearly three months after Antwerp's fall.

By the beginning of November, all seven Allied armies were still positioned in front of the West Wall. Allied hopes of ending the war in 1944 were fading. Each Allied division required 700 tons of sustenance per day and the supply lines stretched 300 to 500 miles back to the Normandy beaches. Yet despite the logistical challenge and the approach of winter, Eisenhower intended to keep on attacking.

The breach of the West Wall at Aachen had convinced the Germans that Eisenhower planned a broader attack toward the Rhine. They were right. The operation would be led by General Bradley. The U.S. First Army, under General Hodges, would advance from Aachen toward Geilenkirchen to reach the Rhine at Cologne. Hodges's left flank would be protected by the U.S. Ninth Army, under Lieut. General William H. Simpson. Simpson would proceed northward between the Maas and Roer rivers to link with Dempsey's British Second Army, attacking southeastward from Nijmegen to create a broad front on the west bank of the Lower Rhine. To the south, the U.S. Third Army would screen the First Army's right flank and drive toward the Saar, while the U.S. Sixth Army Group continued its advance to the upper Rhine near Strasbourg.

Bradley's interim objective was a string of seven dams on the headwaters of the Roer. The Allies feared that the Germans would release the dam waters to flood the Rhine plain. Before going after the dams, however, the Americans wanted to eliminate a threat to their right flank from the Germans holding the Hürtgen Forest, fifteen miles southeast of Aachen. It promised to be a tough fight; the Americans had lost 4,500 men in a failed effort to penetrate the forest in October.

Anticipating the coming attack and struggling under the manpower limits imposed on him by Hitler, Model quickly reshuffled Army Group B, moving the Fifth Panzer and the Seventh armies into defensive positions east of Aachen. His immediate task was clear—to keep the Allies away from the Roer River. Meanwhile, inside the Hürtgen Forest, the Germans had set up a witches' brew of barbed wire entanglements, machine-gun nests, pillboxes, and tens of thousands of mines, many of them mounted in wooden or glass containers in order to foil mine detectors. The thick underbrush and canopy of trees denied the Americans the use of their accustomed air support, and in the cramped setting, the superior American mobility and firepower were nullified.

After a five-day delay imposed by bad weather, the attack began on November 16 with a raid by 2,500 American and British heavy bombers. Infantrymen from the U.S. Ninth and First armies then plunged into the cold, wet woods. Steady rain and sleet made radio communications difficult, and the soldiers' clothing became soaked and frozen. Progress was measured by yards in the seesaw struggle that followed; the village of Hürtgen changed hands no fewer than fourteen times.

The Hürtgen Forest claimed 31,500 American casualties—one of every four men who entered it. Estimated German losses were twice that high. On December 3, the U.S. Ninth Army finally punched through to the Roer at the towns of Jülich and Linnich, but it was another two weeks before the U.S. First Army caught up. The Germans retained control of the Roer dams, and with it the power to release a paralyzing flood across the path of the advance. On December 15, the Americans halted the Roer River offensive.

The bloody month-long fighting had earned them a scant eight miles of

Mobile rocket launchers from the U.S. V Corps fire on German positions in the Hürtgen Forest in late November 1944. During the fierce six-week struggle for the woodland, the Americans suffered 31,500 killed, wounded, or captured and lost another 5,000 to battle fatigue and illness.

German territory. To the southeast, the French First Army of the Sixth Army Group had liberated Strasbourg on November 23 but could go no farther. Patton had made little progress toward the Saar, and the British armies in the northwest were still trying to clear the Netherlands. In addition, Hitler had begun firing his new V-1 flying bombs on Antwerp.

The defensive accomplishments of the Germans—at Arnhem, at Aachen, at the Scheldt, and in the Hürtgen Forest—encouraged the citizens at home and inspired them to laud the autumn recovery as the "miracle of the west." The Allies, for their part, had absorbed a bitter lesson regarding the defensive abilities of the German army. Now, in what they so recently had hoped would be the final year of the conflict, the Allies would receive yet

another painful lesson about the offensive strength of the Wehrmacht.

Adolf Hitler's unlikely plan for a massive counterstroke had been taking shape ever since the Allies had driven his armies from France. Evaluating possible routes of attack, he had settled on the Ardennes, a heavily forested mountain range between Luxembourg and Belgium. It was a hostile place of steep ravines, thick tree cover, deeply cut rivers, and few roads or trails. The German extension of the Ardennes, the Eifel Forest, provided excellent cover for assembling the necessary forces.

In September, Hitler secretly directed that orders covering the 1940 blitzkrieg through the same region be retrieved from an archive at Liegnitz.

German soldiers hastily evacuate Strasbourg, the economic and cultural capital of Alsace, on November 22, 1944. The next day, the French 2d Division liberated the city that Hitler had incorporated into the Reich in 1940 after the conquest of France.

On October 9, OKW operations chief Jodl presented a sketch of the plan for a similar offensive with the misleading code name *Wacht am Rhein* (Watch on the Rhine). With the Allied forces unevenly spread out in a 400-mile-long chain, Hitler saw a great opportunity—he would deliver a crippling blow at its weakest link in the dead of the coming winter, when an attack would be least suspected. On October 29, he telephoned Joseph Goebbels to wish his propaganda chief a happy birthday. The Führer assured Goebbels that by Christmas everything would be changed. The German people, he said, could look forward to receiving a "great military triumph" as their Christmas gift for 1944.

The fighting in the Aachen sector served as a perfect screen for the gathering of powerful German forces west of the Rhine. All orders for Operation Watch on the Rhine began with the deceptive statement: "In light of the anticipated enemy offensive," as though the Germans were preparing their defenses to prevent an Allied breakthrough across the great river barrier. Under this cover, Hitler began assembling the Sixth SS Panzer Army in the area around Cologne during the November fighting. To command this new force, he selected the loyal SS General Josef "Sepp" Dietrich. A butcher by trade, Dietrich had proved an able and courageous soldier who enjoyed the complete trust of the troops. He had risen through the ranks and had commanded the crack Liebstandarte Adolf Hitler Division on the eastern front.

Allied Intelligence puzzled as to why the new army had not been brought in to blunt their attacks on the Roer. Hitler kept them guessing with a number of other confusing moves. He transferred General Manteuffel's Fifth Panzer Army headquarters staff from Army Group G to Army Group B, sending them into line behind Aachen supposedly to prepare defensive works. To relieve Model of some of his burdens as he prepared Army Group B for Operation Watch on the Rhine, Hitler created a new Army Group H, under General Student, consisting of the Fifteenth Army and the First Paratroop Army in Holland. Hitler then quietly removed Manteuffel's headquarters staff from the Aachen area, replacing them with the headquarters staff of Zangen's Fifteenth Army, disguised under the name Group Manteuffel. The headquarters staff of the Armed Forces Netherlands then stepped into Zangen's vacant command in Holland, assuming the name of the Fifteenth Army. Manteuffel's headquarters staff, meanwhile, under the cover name Military Police Command for Special Assignment, focused its attention on preparing for the counteroffensive.

The prevailing Allied assumption that the German army in the west was no longer capable of serious offensive action held firm. Hitler's winter surprise was on track. All planning, preparations, and orders for the coun-

teroffensive, one OKW diarist noted, remained in the hands of the Führer, including even the daily decisions to supply various numbers of vehicles and horses to individual units. As Manteuffel observed: "The plan for the Ardennes offensive was drawn up completely by OKW and sent to us as a cut-and-dried 'Führer directive.'"

The directive called for a three-pronged attack: the Sixth SS Panzer Army, under Dietrich; the Fifth Panzer Army, under Manteuffel; and the Seventh Army, under Brandenberger. Hitler assigned the main task to Dietrich. The Sixth SS Panzer would attack northwestward through the Ardennes Forest, cross the Meuse between Liége and Huy, and drive for Antwerp. Manteuffel's army would make a long northwesterly sweep, along Dietrich's southern flank, crossing the Meuse between Namur and Dinant, and advancing on Brussels. The Seventh Army, meanwhile, would race for the Meuse on the Germans' extreme southern flank.

Hitler expected the attack to deprive the Allies of their most vital port, split the Anglo-American front, and isolate the British army, forcing it to withdraw from the Continent. He counted on the element of surprise to permit his forces to accomplish all of these lofty objectives in just seven days. A rapid victory was needed "before the French should begin to conscript their manpower." As for the exact date of the operation, Hitler said, the "weather and he would decide that."

The Führer left his senior generals sputtering with objections when they met to review the plan at Model's headquarters. Antwerp was 125 miles away, they pointed out. Even if the German armies could fight their way to the city and retake it, they would be unable to hold the ground covered by the advance. Moreover, the generals considered it foolhardy to concentrate the bulk of the supplies and reserves on the Sixth SS Panzer Army when the Fifth Panzer Army had the greater distance to travel. They further noted that the 1940 blitzkreig that carried the Germans all the way to the English Channel had been accomplished with forty-four divisions, eventually growing to seventy-one. Now, against a much stronger foe, Hitler proposed doing the same thing with the equivalent of twenty-eight divisions, only nine of which were armored.

"Hitler was clearly trying to resurrect in miniature the basic concept of the offensive in the west of May 1940," complained OKW deputy chief of operations, General Walther Warlimont, "although the miniature was far too large for the existing circumstances."

Still, Hitler's counterstroke had many commendable features. The three German armies would mass more than 240,000 soldiers to attack an area defended by no more than 80,000. In addition, the assault would occur at a time and place that the enemy never expected. And even if it did not deal the Allies a crippling blow, it would buy time to allow the Germans to rebuild their bombed-out factories and build more V-2 rockets, jet fighter planes, and modernized U-boats—the new superweapons that Hitler claimed would win the war.

Rundstedt, who had not been consulted by Hitler or OKW during the planning, called the plan a "stroke of genius," but entirely too ambitious. The commander in chief West knew that protesting was useless, given that the Führer had marked the orders in his own handwriting, "Not to be altered." Nor was Rundstedt mollified when Jodl told him candidly that the "daring concept of the aim was unalterable, an aim that, looked at from a purely technical point of view, seems out of keeping with the forces allotted: None should be daunted on this account, however, and all must be staked on a single card."

Working together, Rundstedt and Model proposed an alternative plan. Called the Small Solution, it aimed simply at pinching off the American salient at Aachen and seizing an Allied supply base at Liége. Model made several attempts to dissuade Hitler from targeting Antwerp as the goal of the operation, but the Führer brushed aside his pleas, deriding Model's Small Solution as a "half solution."

Hitler pointed out that the generals had consistently been wrong during the autumn battles. They had warned that the West Wall would collapse if it were not reinforced; it had not. They had said he could not create more reserves, yet four new Volksgrenadier divisions had tasted battle in November. They had complained of equipment shortages, yet more than 1,300 new or repaired tanks had arrived in the west in November, with 1,000 more expected soon. They complained of lack of air support, but Himmler promised to have 1,500 planes available for the operation, including 100 new jet fighters. In addition, Hitler had managed to sequester more than 4.2 million gallons of gasoline and fifty trainloads of ammunition.

Only Manteuffel was able to make headway in getting the Führer to reconsider any aspect of the plan. He pointed out to Model that by launching the offensive with artillery at 7:30 a.m. and attacking at 11:00 a.m., the Germans would be giving away the element of surprise and limiting themselves to five hours of daylight before darkness ended the short winter days. Launching the forward ground units at 5:30 a.m. without an artillery prelude would give the shock troops a better chance to achieve a deep penetration of the enemy positions.

Model quite agreed with Manteuffel, but cautioned him, "You had better argue it out with the Führer."

"All right, I'll do that if you'll come with me," Manteuffel replied. On December 2, after a five-hour meeting in Berlin, Hitler consented. That, in

addition to changing the operation's name to that of Model's Small Solution—*Herbstnebel* (Autumn Mist)—was his only concession.

The winter weather set in early. After a heavy snow in mid-November, rain followed sleet and continued cold; fog covered the tree tops. Most corps and division commanders remained ignorant of the plan until later in the month, giving them scant time to study the terrain they would fight over. When Model visited a corps headquarters, several officers complained that supplies were short and that too many obstacles lay in the path of the attack. The combative field marshal exploded at what he considered defeatism, snapping, "If you need anything, take it from the Americans!"

Rundstedt reported to OKW that his forces were 3,500 officers and 115,000 men short of desirable levels. He complained that the efficiency of the reinforcement divisions was poor because their training had been too

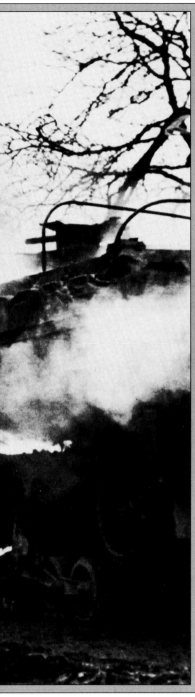

Panzergrenadiers of the 2d SS Panzer Division pass a line of burning American vehicles near a vital road junction at Manhay, Belgium. The German troops captured the village on December 24, 1944, opening a route westward toward the Meuse.

brief. Hitler ignored Rundstedt's gloomy messages. He was too busy briefing General Student on the role his paratroopers were to play and in working out plans with SS Lieut. Colonel Otto Skorzeny, the daring commando leader who in 1943 had brought off the spectacular rescue of deposed Italian dictator Benito Mussolini. Skorzeny would train a commando force of English-speaking Germans to pass for American soldiers. Disguised in American uniforms and driving captured jeeps, they would sow confusion and spread terror behind enemy lines. Hitler called Skorzeny's special mission Operation *Greif,* or Griffin, for the mythical half-eagle, half-lion creature of that name.

On December 12, Hitler summoned his senior commanders to Rundstedt's headquarters for a final look at the plan. Wary of betrayal, he ordered the generals stripped of their side arms and briefcases before entering a bunker that was guarded by double rows of burly SS officers. The generals took their seats with an SS guard standing over their shoulders behind each chair. Then the Führer entered. He looked, one general noted, "old and broken, and his hand shook as he read from a long prepared manuscript."

Hitler lectured the senior commanders for nearly two hours. "Never in history," he declared, "was there a coalition like that of our enemies, composed of such heterogeneous elements with such divergent aims. Ultra-capitalist states on the one hand; ultra-Marxist states on the other. On one hand, a dying empire, Britain; on the other, a colony bent upon inheritance, the United States. Even now these states are at loggerheads, and he who, like a spider sitting in the middle of his web, can watch developments, observes how these antagonisms grow stronger and stronger from hour to hour. If now we can deliver a few more heavy blows, then at any moment this artificially bolstered common front may suddenly collapse with a gigantic clap of thunder."

Even the skeptical Montgomery, in mid-December, sent a rosy assessment to his troops: "The enemy is at present fighting a defensive campaign on all fronts; his situation is such that he cannot stage major offensive operations." Although Rundstedt had been nothing but a figurehead for months, his presence as commander in chief West helped confuse the Allies. Based on their knowledge of his previous behavior, they assumed that the cautious sixty-nine-year-old theater commander was holding back his strongest forces to defend the West Wall and the Rhine.

The American command, busily attacking or preparing to attack along the flatter avenues into Germany, had confidently thinned its forces in the Ardennes. Two of the five divisions posted there had little or no combat experience, and the other two were resting and refitting after their ordeal in the Hürtgen Forest. Despite the German success in using the Ardennes

as a highway in 1940, the American senior commanders still considered the region impassable to large armored forces.

Orders sent out from OKW scheduled Operation Autumn Mist for December 10. Then Hitler postponed the launch until the 14th to allow more time for the troops to reach their jumping-off positions. They moved over the Eifel's winding mountain roads, which had been covered with straw in order to muffle the rumble of armor and the sound of the hoofbeats of the horses that were drawing vehicles. Another postponement followed, with the new and final date set for December 16. Hitler informed Model that OKW had sent out the final orders and that they were to be carried out to the last detail. Model confirmed that he had received the orders and had relayed them to Dietrich "word for word." Jodl then dispatched the message: "The final decisions have been made; everything points to victory."

Cloaked in the foggy darkness of December 16, at 5:30 a.m., the Ardennes offensive roared into motion against an unsuspecting enemy, powered by fully half of the German forces available on the western front. As the troops and vehicles sprang forward, 1,900 guns began a ninety-minute bombardment of the American positions in front of them, and V-1 flying bombs and V-2 rockets screamed toward their targets in Liége and Antwerp.

A lieutenant in the 12th SS Panzer (Hitlerjugend) Division described the moment in a letter to his sister: "I write during one of the momentous hours before we attack, full of excitement and expectation of what the next days will bring. Some believe in living, but life is not everything! It is enough to know that we attack and will throw the enemy from our homeland. It is a holy task. Above me is the terrific noise of V-1s and artillery, the voice of war." Meanwhile, inside the Reich, propaganda minister Joseph Goebbels exulted over the Radio Berlin airwaves: "The Wehrmacht has launched its great offensive. We will destroy the enemy and cut all his lines of communication. Paris is our goal!"

The Allies were slow to perceive the magnitude of the attack. "My storm battalions infiltrated rapidly into the American front—like raindrops," Manteuffel would recall. General Bradley assumed that it was merely a spoiling action. Eisenhower waited a full day before mobilizing the 82d and 101st Airborne divisions out of reserve at Rheims, France. Hitler had

SS Lieut. Colonel Otto Skorzeny *(above, left)* salutes at a Nazi gathering. Hitler chose the scar-faced master commando to train English-speaking saboteurs to sow confusion in American rear areas during the opening hours of the Ardennes counteroffensive. Driving captured jeeps and wearing American uniforms, seven of Skorzeny's teams infiltrated U.S. lines. Eighteen of the men were caught and executed by firing squad, as were the three above at Henri-Chapelle. Other German soldiers who had replaced their uniforms with American issue also paid a price: Those who fell into American hands often were summarily shot, like the SS man at right.

achieved his surprise. Even the weather favored the Germans. For an entire week, dense fog and short periods of daylight hampered Allied aerial reconnaissance and tactical air support.

Skorzeny's commandos, who had penetrated the American lines from the southern boundary of the Sixth SS Panzer Army, enjoyed a brief measure of success. Although most were quickly caught, their very existence created traffic jams, as nervous sentries in search of the imposters quizzed their fellow Americans on such trivia as the names of major-league baseball teams, movie stars, and the husband of pinup girl Betty Grable. After one captured commando claimed that he was on a mission to assassinate Eisenhower, the Allied supreme commander was put under close guard at his Paris headquarters.

The primary German strike force, Sepp Dietrich's Sixth SS Panzer Army, consisted of five infantry divisions and four armored divisions with a total of about 450 tanks, including 90 new sixty-eight-ton Royal Tigers. On the right flank, four of the SS-trained Volksgrenadier infantry divisions, attacking from north of the Eifel, were assigned to capture the towns of Monschau and Butgenbach in order to open the road leading west. Many of the soldiers were veterans of winter fighting in Russia. They wore white capes so that they would blend with the snow-covered terrain. (Once they recovered from the shock of the surprise attack, the Americans had to requisition Belgian bedsheets for camouflage.)

At Monschau, elements of the U.S. 2d and 99th Infantry divisions blocked the road. A unit of 1,000 German paratroopers, led by Lieut. Colonel Friedrich Baron von der Heydte, set out to clear the roadways for the ground troops. But most of the Luftwaffe's battle-worn Ju-52 and Ju-88 transports ferrying them into battle never made it to the drop zone. Flown by inexperienced pilots, many of them strayed off course, and others were shot down by American antiaircraft fire. Only about 300 paratroopers landed safely, and they were soon isolated and captured by the Americans.

The I Panzer Corps on Dietrich's left flank fared better. Spearheaded by Task Force Peiper, under the command of fanatical twenty-nine-year-old SS Lieut. Colonel Joachim Peiper, it consisted of 2,000 veteran troops and 120 tanks. After breaking through the Losheim Gap, the task force headed westward, reaching the town of Stavelot on December 18—just a few miles from the U.S. First Army headquarters at the town of Spa and even closer to two huge fuel dumps containing three million gallons of gasoline. On December 24, out of fuel and surrounded by the U.S. 30th Division, which had rushed down from Aachen, Peiper and 800 of his men escaped on foot, leaving behind 39 tanks and a bloody trail of murdered American prisoners of war and Belgian civilians. News of the massacres spread quickly among the American forces, prompting some GIs to vow that they would never again take prisoners in SS uniforms.

Assigned to capture the vital road junctions of Saint-Vith and Bastogne en route to the Meuse, Manteuffel's Fifth Panzer Army made the deepest penetration, driving sixty miles into the American lines on a thirty-mile-wide front. On December 19, the Fifth Panzer surrounded two regiments of the U.S. 106th Infantry Division in the Schnee Eifel, forcing the surrender of 8,000 men—the largest number of Americans captured in a single day in the European theater. The 2d Panzer Division of General Smilo von Lüttwitz's XLVII Panzer Corps reached as far west as Celles, only four miles from the Meuse, creating an ugly protrusion on Allied battle maps. It was the contours of this salient that gave Hitler's Ardennes offensive its name in American annals—the Battle of the Bulge.

After a slow early reaction, the Allied command sensed the scope of the German counterstroke. Eisenhower shuffled his forces up and down the West Wall and brought Patton's Third Army up from the Saar to Belgium. On December 19, he halted all offensive operations north and south of the Ardennes and committed 335,000 Americans to thwarting Hitler's attack.

On Christmas Eve, Manteuffel proposed to Hitler that he make a circular strike northward on the east side of the Meuse, using reserves from OKW and the Sixth SS Panzer Army. Time was short and Manteuffel insisted on receiving a reply that night. Earlier in the battle, the Führer had refused a request by Manteuffel for a mechanized division from the Seventh Army, and he was still reluctant to give up a central role for his ideologically pure Sixth SS Panzer Army. Nonetheless, he relented, switching the main offensive role to Manteuffel and abandoning hopes for regaining Antwerp. Now the German target was the Meuse.

Manteuffel immediately began an assault on the crossroads town of Bastogne. The 2d Panzer and the 26th Volksgrenadier divisions had already linked up with the Panzer Lehr Division to ring the town, trapping a unit of the 101st Airborne Division and parts of the 9th and 10th Armored divisions, all under the command of Brigadier General Anthony C. McAuliffe. On December 22, Lüttwitz had dispatched a white-flag party to the Americans to demand a surrender. McAuliffe, who was not given to profanity, uttered a reply for the history books: "Nuts." (Confused at first by the literal translation, Lüttwitz was finally told by his interpreters that it meant something akin to the expression: "Go to hell!")

Model persuaded Hitler to allow him to send Manteuffel reinforcements for a renewed assault on Bastogne. The Luftwaffe aircraft that had been specially set aside for the counteroffensive bombed the besieged city on Christmas Eve, and ground forces attacked Christmas Day. But the Amer-

icans held on grimly until Patton's U.S. Third Army armor, racing northward through snow and darkness, broke the German ring the next day and relieved Bastogne. The reserves that Manteuffel had requested finally arrived in late December, but by then, his tanks and trucks were out of gas and stranded along a line 100 miles long.

Manteuffel telephoned Jodl and told him to inform Hitler that he was going to withdraw his lead units. Hitler forbade it. "So instead of withdrawing in time," Manteuffel said, "we were driven back bit by bit under pressure of the Allied attacks, suffering needlessly." It was at this point that the Fifth Panzer Army ran out of medals. Soldiers cited for bravery now received an autographed photograph of Rundstedt—a poor substitute for the Iron Cross. One division commander suggested that a more fitting award would be a few days of leave.

The fighting dragged on into January. In the last days of December, clear

These pictures show a combat moment during the drive across Belgium by Task Force Peiper, the spearhead of the Sixth SS Panzer Army, led by SS Lieut. Colonel Joachim Peiper *(top left, wearing hooded overcoat)*. During the fighting for Stoumont on December 19, an American shell scores a direct hit on Peiper's lead Panther tank *(far left)*. Shielded by the burning tank, a German squad sets up a machine gun *(above)*, while a comrade *(left)* retrieves a Panzerfaust antitank weapon. After capturing Stoumont and two nearby villages, the task force ran out of fuel and was boxed in by the U.S. 30th Infantry Division. Peiper and most of his men escaped through the lines, leaving a trail of massacred civilians and American POWs. In 1946, a war crimes tribunal sentenced him to death but later reprieved him for lack of evidence. Peiper burned to death in 1976, after unknown assailants set fire to his home in eastern France.

weather allowed Allied air power to overwhelm the battered German armored divisions, despite a surprise attack by a large force of Luftwaffe fighters on New Year's Day that destroyed 156 Allied planes on the ground, including Montgomery's private aircraft.

On January 3, the Allies counterattacked. Rundstedt recommended a complete withdrawal. Hitler, as usual, refused. A few days later, however, he pulled out the Sixth SS Panzer Army, dispatching it to Hungary. On January 8, he reluctantly agreed to bring the remaining German forces back behind the relative safety of the West Wall.

"We now had to pay for our tardiness in retiring from the great salient," Manteuffel recalled. "The exhausted condition of our troops had been underestimated at Supreme Headquarters. They were more tired even than we had expected, and were no longer capable, either physically or mentally, of coping with a tough, well-equipped, and well-fed army."

The Ardennes counteroffensive, in the words of Rundstedt, had turned into "Stalingrad no. 2." The Germans had inflicted 81,000 casualties on the Allies—nearly all of them American—and destroyed about 800 Allied tanks in the biggest battle of the western front. But they had lost 100,000 men, 800 tanks, and 1,000 aircraft.

Hitler tried to put these terrible losses in the best possible light. As epilogue to his failed master stroke, he told his generals that although the counteroffensive had "not resulted in the decisive success that might have been expected, a tremendous easing of the situation has come about. The enemy has had to abandon all his plans for attack."

Nothing could have been farther from the truth. Hitler's great Ardennes gamble had consumed much of the manpower and armaments he needed to mount a firm defense of German soil. And with all hope of a triumphant coup in the West gone aglimmer, the Germans would find no comfort in turning to the east, where the Soviet war machine was poised once again to roll toward Berlin.

But the Führer never lost his optimism. Describing the Reich's current misfortunes as "nothing new in history," he again sought solace in the writings of his hero, Frederick the Great. "Only now I was reading through a volume of letters," he explained to a trusted aide. The Führer then quoted a passage penned by the Prussian soldier-king in 1759, the blackest period of the Seven Years' War: "There was a time when I went on campaign with the most magnificent army in Europe. Now, I have a heap of rubble—I possess no commanders, my generals are no longer proper leaders, and my troops are of appalling quality."

"You cannot imagine a more devastating indictment," said Hitler, "and yet this man stuck it out through the war." And so would he. ✠

Battles for Control of the West

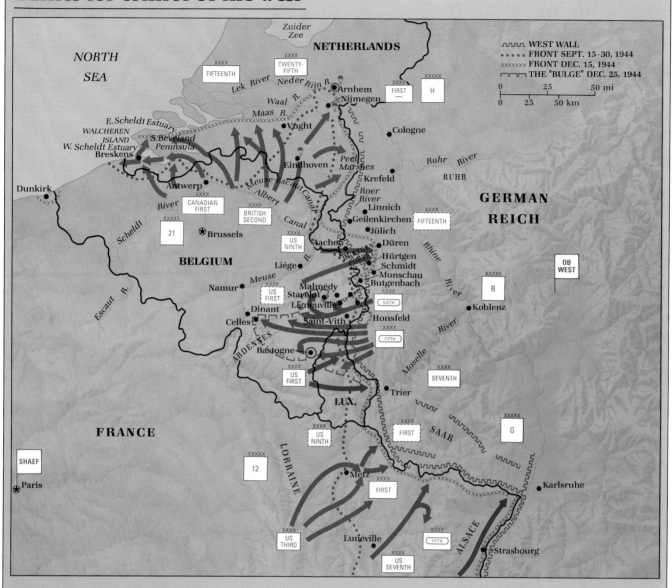

NORTH SEA

Zuider Zee

NETHERLANDS

Lek River
Neder Rijn R.
Waal R.
Maas R.
E. Scheldt Estuary
WALCHEREN ISLAND
S. Beveland Peninsula
W. Scheldt Estuary
Breskens
Dunkirk
Antwerp
Albert Canal
Meuse-Escaut Canal
Canal
Scheldt
BELGIUM
Brussels
Namur
Meuse
Escaut R.
FRANCE
SHAEF
Paris

Arnhem
Nijmegen
Vught
Eindhoven
Peel Marshes
Krefeld
Roer River
Linnich
Geilenkirchen
Jülich
Düren
Aachen
HÜRTGEN FOREST
Liége
Hürtgen
Schmidt
Monschau
Butgenbach
Malmédy
Stavelot
Ligneuville
Dinant
Saint-Vith
Honsfeld
Celles
Bastogne
ARDENNES
LUX.
Trier
Metz
LORRAINE
Lunéville
SAAR
Strasbourg
ALSACE
Karlsruhe
Koblenz
Moselle River
Rhine River
Ruhr River
RUHR
Cologne

GERMAN REICH

WEST WALL
FRONT SEPT. 15-30, 1944
FRONT DEC. 15, 1944
THE "BULGE" DEC. 25, 1944

0   25   50 mi
0   25   50 km

FIFTEENTH
TWENTY-FIFTH
FIRST   H
CANADIAN FIRST
21
BRITISH SECOND
US NINTH
FIFTEENTH
US FIRST
SIXTH
B
OB WEST
FIFTH
US FIRST
SEVENTH
FIRST
G
US NINTH
12
FIRST
US THIRD
FIFTH
US SEVENTH

During the fall of 1944, the Allies initiated a number of exhausting offensives aimed at surmounting the West Wall. These attacks set the stage for Hitler's last great gamble—a surprise counteroffensive through the rugged Ardennes Forest of Luxembourg and Belgium. In September, Operation Market-Garden sought to outflank the West Wall by dropping paratroopers behind the German lines. The paratroopers were to seize vital bridges at Eindhoven, Nijmegen, and Arnhem and join ground forces advancing from Belgium, sixty miles to the south. Bad weather and stiff German resistance prevented the linkup at Arnhem, forcing an end to the operation. Throughout October and November, the Americans continued to advance toward the Rhine, capturing Aachen on October 21 and Metz on November 22. On December 3, they reached the Roer River, after a bloody, six-week struggle in the Hürtgen Forest. While these battles raged, Hitler secretly amassed a powerful strike force west of the Rhine. On December 16, he launched his counteroffensive against a lightly defended section of the Ardennes front. The attack aimed at capturing the Allied logistical base at Antwerp and cutting off the forces to the north. The Fifth Panzer Army made the deepest penetration in the Allied lines, advancing to within four miles of the Meuse. But the Germans could go no farther and were soon on the defensive again.

Hitler's Army of Last Resort

On September 25, 1944, shortly after the ground fighting reached German soil for the first time, Adolf Hitler ordered the formation of a *Volkssturm*, or People's Army. The idea of scraping the bottom of the barrel to create a home defense force out of Germany's last remaining pool of manpower had been proposed by General Heinz Guderian, chief of the army general staff, in July following the collapse of Army Group Center on the eastern front. But it was not until Martin Bormann, the Führer's private secretary and éminence grise, snatched the idea for his own that Hitler acceded to it. "Today, after some labor pains, the Führer consented to the Volkssturm order," Bormann confided to his wife. "I feel like a new mother, exhausted but happy."

Hitler's decree automatically made every semi-healthy male civilian between the ages of sixteen and sixty a member of the new force. Under Bormann's leadership, the gauleiters, or Nazi district leaders, set up induction centers in every town and village in the Reich. They mobilized more than one million men and boys. This unpromising cadre, called an "army of idealists" by Bormann, included veterans who had been invalided out of the service, old men hitherto considered unfit for even limited duty, and highly indoctrinated teenagers. To maximize the propaganda impact, the Volkssturm was inaugurated on October 18, the anniversary of the 1813 Battle of the Nations, when the armies of the German states and their foreign allies defeated Napoleon at Leipzig.

Reichsführer-SS Heinrich Himmler, in his capacity as commander in chief of the Reserve Army, supervised military training and provided arms and equipment. With most Volkssturm members working long hours in various war industries, Sunday was generally the only day of the week when they could drill. There was no official uniform. Many members trained with nothing more than a dummy rifle and an armband.

Although Volkssturm units were supposed to serve only near their hometowns, many ended up on battlefronts, where they were ill-prepared to fight. The older men often slipped away to safety, but many of the youngsters died fighting fanatically.

Paunchy Volkssturm volunteers parade past Heinrich Himmler,

Heinz Guderian, and gauleiter Arthur Greisler in Poznan. The recruiting poster (*inset*) reads "For Freedom and Life."

Basic Training
for Weekend
Warriors

An elderly Volkssturm volunteer
gingerly examines an 1890-
vintage Austrian rifle that he
has been issued. The weapon
was obsolete as early as the
beginning of World War I.

A middle-aged recruit flinches
after firing a practice round
with a *Panzerfaust* antitank
weapon. Other members of his
unit await their turns to fire.

A teenager prepares to
hurl a stick grenade as his
amused instructor, a senior
Luftwaffe officer, points in
the direction of the target.

Lying in a trench, a group of youths practice reading military compasses under close observation by their instructors.

Volkssturm members from the Moselle region of Germany learn the workings of a machine gun. The mustached man explaining the gun's operation is the father of the boy at left.

Unlikely Defenders Armed for Battle

A bespectacled youngster wearing the Volkssturm armband over his Hitler Youth uniform inserts a grenade into the holster of a Storm Trooper. Other unit members carry Panzerfaust antitank weapons and an assortment of outdated rifles.

Dwarfed by their outsize overcoats and weighed down by their weapons, two Volkssturm youths lumber off to the front, little suspecting the horrors of real war that await them.

TWO

Disaster on Two Fronts

eneral Heinz Guderian, the fifty-six-year-old tank specialist who had become chief of the general staff of the army high command (OKH) after the July 20 attempt on Adolf Hitler's life, had never been a political general. The broadfaced, Prussian-born Guderian was a no-nonsense soldier, as blunt and effective as the panzers he commanded during the war's early years. In his new capacity, he was the same straightforward battler he had always been—some said he had grown even more stubborn—but his battles now were most often with his own commander in chief.

Guderian's mission when he arrived at the Adlerhorst, Hitler's western front headquarters in central Hesse, on Christmas Eve 1944 was to convince the Führer that the Ardennes offensive had stalled and that every available German division should be rushed to Poland and East Prussia where the Soviets were massing the largest buildup of the war. As Guderian saw it, the imminent Russian attack meant nothing less than life or death for the Third Reich. Guderian urged Hitler to shift troops not only from the western front but also from Norway and the Balkans. He also asked permission to evacuate General Ferdinand Schörner's Army Group North from the Courland peninsula (present-day western Latvia) where it was pinned against the Baltic Sea by the Soviet First and Second Baltic fronts, or army groups. With stronger armored reserves, he reasoned, the German forces in Poland and East Prussia could fight the war of movement that was their only chance of survival.

Hitler listened as Guderian ticked off the estimates of enemy strength: In infantry the Soviet advantage was eleven to one, in tanks seven to one, in artillery twenty to one. Even with an infusion of forces from other sectors, the odds against the Germans were forbidding. But Hitler refused to accept either the numbers or Guderian's urgent recommendations. The buildup, he declared, was the "greatest bluff since Genghis Khan."

Guderian stubbornly persisted, but the Führer would hear none of it. The army chief of staff remembered Hitler's boast made during another such meeting not long before: "There is no need for you to try to teach me," Hitler had said. "I have been commanding the German army in the field for five

With Soviet guns booming in the distance, terror-stricken civilians laden with their belongings flee Königsberg, the capital of East Prussia. Their desperate flight was spurred by the knowledge that the approaching Red Army was under orders to take brutal revenge against the entire German nation.

years, and during that time I have had more practical experience than any 'gentleman' of the general staff could ever hope to have." Heinrich Himmler echoed his leader during the Christmas Eve dinner at the Adlerhorst. "The figures are grossly exaggerated," the Reichsführer-SS told Guderian solemnly. "I am convinced there is nothing going on in the east."

What was in fact going on was precisely what Guderian feared. For months, Stavka, the Soviet high command, had been planning a winter offensive that would take advantage of the Red Army's overwhelming superiority in numbers and equipment. The huge, sweeping operation would take place in central Poland on the frozen, 180-mile-wide plain between Warsaw and the Carpathian Mountains, a section of the front that was defended by Army Group A, under the command of General Josef Harpe.

The attack would develop out of three bridgeheads that the Soviets had established the previous summer on the banks of the Vistula River: a forty-five-mile-wide bridgehead at Baranow, held by Marshal Ivan S. Konev's First Ukrainian Front; and two smaller bridgeheads to the north, at Pulawy and Magnuszew, held by the First Belorussian Front of Marshal Georgy K. Zhukov. After bursting out of Baranow, Konev intended to split his forces, sending one wing northwestward to help Zhukov clear the cities of Kielce and Radom, while the other wing plunged southwestward toward Krakow and Upper Silesia. Zhukov's forces at Pulawy would advance on Lodz while his forces at Magnuszew attacked Kutno and Warsaw. After achieving their initial objectives, both fronts would link up and drive straight for the Oder River and Berlin. If all went according to plan, Stavka expected the grand offensive to end the war in forty-five days.

Soviet engineers had begun laying the groundwork for the Vistula-Oder operation in September by converting the railways in eastern Poland to the wider Russian gauge and by building parallel sets of roads to the front-line divisions. By early January of 1945, the combined forces of Konev and Zhukov had amassed a total of 2.2 million soldiers, 6,400 tanks and assault guns, and 46,000 pieces of artillery. In contrast, General Harpe's Army Group A, which consisted of the German Ninth, Seventeenth, and Fourth Panzer armies, could count on only 400,000 men, 4,100 artillery pieces, and 1,150 tanks and assault guns—a deficit nearly as lopsided as Guderian's intelligence estimates.

Stavka designed secondary offensives on both flanks to assist the main drive to Berlin. On the southern flank, south of the Carpathians in Hungary, the Soviets were already engaged in heavy fighting with General Otto Wöhler's Army Group South around Budapest, which the Red Army had encircled on December 26. On the northern flank, in northern Poland and

General Heinz Guderian, chief of the army general staff, hurries into the Reich Chancellery during the winter of 1945. Guderian regularly spent up to three hours each day driving back and forth between his OKH headquarters at Zossen and Berlin to comply with Hitler's demand for twice-daily briefings on the status of the war on the eastern front.

East Prussia, Stavka planned to break up and isolate General Hans Reinhardt's Army Group Center. Reinhardt's line wound from the Bay of Courland in the northeast south to a position just above Warsaw. General Konstantin K. Rokossovsky's Second Belorussian Front would break out of its bridgeheads on the Narew River at Serock and Rozan and drive northwest against the Fourth and Second armies, racing for the Baltic coast on either side of Danzig. To Rokossovsky's right, the Third Belorussian Front, under General Ivan D. Chernyakovsky, would attack south from its Pregel River base and assault Königsberg, the ancient capital of East Prussia, separating the Third Panzer Army from the rest of Army Group Center while also sealing off the Fourth Army in the Masurian Lakes region.

Together, Rokossovsky and Chernyakovsky commanded 1.7 million troops, nearly three times more than Reinhardt. With 3,300 tanks and assault guns, 28,000 artillery pieces, and vast stocks of fuel and ammunition, the Soviets enjoyed an even greater edge in mobility and firepower.

While the Soviets completed their final deployments, Guderian made two more trips to the Adlerhorst. Before seeing Hitler on New Year's Day, he extracted an assurance from the commander in chief West, Field Marshal Gerd von Rundstedt, that four divisions were available for transfer to Poland and East Prussia. But Hitler trumped him by ordering the divisions to Hungary. On January 9, in anticipation of the Russian offensive, Guderian asked permission to pull both Army Group A and Army Group Center back several miles to shorten their defense lines, and again he pleaded for reinforcements. Hitler, spurning both requests, screamed that whoever made OKH's intelligence reports should be in a lunatic asylum.

Stalin had originally planned to launch the offensive on January 20. When British prime minister Winston S. Churchill urged him to move earlier to relieve the pressure in the west, however, the Soviet leader advanced the date to January 12. To keep the Germans off balance, the attack would begin as a sequence of blows, first from Konev at the southern end of the front, then from Chernyakovsky at the northern end, and finally from Zhukov and Rokossovsky.

The morning of January 12 was cold and cloudy, the temperature a few degrees above freezing, and the fog thick enough to keep aircraft on the ground. The guns at the Baranow bridgehead, arrayed in concentrations as dense as 420 pieces per mile, opened fire before dawn on preregistered targets. The Fourth Panzer Army was taken by surprise; the Germans had expected the Russians to wait for the skies to clear in order to have the support of the Soviet air force.

The thunderous bombardment cut the German communications lines and ripped huge holes in the defenses, manned by three infantry divisions.

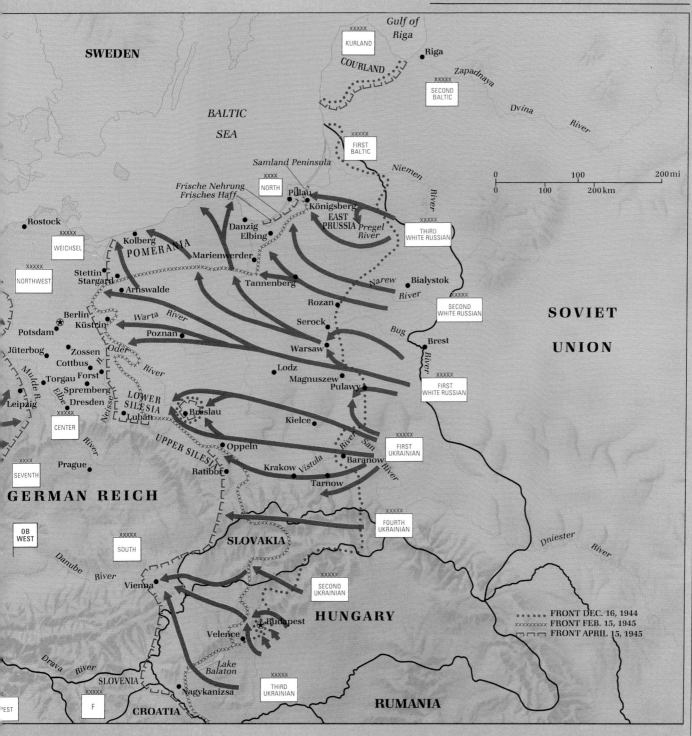

SWEDEN

Gulf of Riga

XXXXX KURLAND

Riga

COURLAND

Zapadnaya

XXXXX SECOND BALTIC

Dvina

River

BALTIC

SEA

Samland Peninsula

XXXXX FIRST BALTIC

Niemen

River

Frische Nehrung
Frisches Haff

XXXX NORTH

Pillau

Königsberg

EAST PRUSSIA

Pregel River

XXXXX THIRD WHITE RUSSIAN

Rostock

XXXXX WEICHSEL

Kolberg

POMERANIA

Danzig

Elbing

Marienwerder

SOVIET

UNION

Stettin

Stargard

XXXXX NORTHWEST

Arnswalde

Tannenberg

Narew

River

Bialystok

Berlin

Küstrin

Potsdam

Warta River

Poznan

Rozan

Serock

Bug

XXXXX SECOND WHITE RUSSIAN

Warsaw

Brest

Jüterbog

Zossen

Cottbus

Forst

Oder

River

Mulde R.

Torgau

Spremberg

Dresden

Elbe R.

LOWER SILESIA

Luban

Neisse River

Breslau

Lodz

Magnuszew

Pulawy

River

Bug

River

XXXXX FIRST WHITE RUSSIAN

Leipzig

XXXXX CENTER

Kielce

River San

XXXXX FIRST UKRAINIAN

UPPER SILESIA

Oppeln

Prague

XXXX SEVENTH

Ratibor

Krakow

Vistula

Baranow

San River

Tarnow

GERMAN REICH

OB WEST

XXXXX SOUTH

SLOVAKIA

XXXXX FOURTH UKRAINIAN

Dniester

River

Danube River

Vienna

XXXXX SECOND UKRAINIAN

Velence

Budapest

HUNGARY

FRONT DEC. 16, 1944
FRONT FEB. 15, 1945
FRONT APRIL 15, 1945

Drava River

SLOVENIA

Nagykanizsa

Lake Balaton

XXXXX THIRD UKRAINIAN

F

CROATIA

RUMANIA

0   100   200 mi
0   100   200 km

By early January of 1945, the Red Army had completed the largest buildup of the war and lay poised for a massive offensive that would carry them all the way to the Oder and Neisse rivers and the final assault on Berlin. The primary Soviet thrust, directed at General Josef Harpe's Army Group A in Poland, sprang out of three bridgeheads on the Vistula River: at Baranow, by the First Ukrainian Front of Marshal Ivan S. Konev; and at Pulawy and Magnuszew, by Marshal Georgy K. Zhukov's First Belorussian Front. To the north, the Second and Third Belorussian fronts launched supporting attacks to trap General Hans Reinhardt's Army Group Center in East Prussia. Soviet fronts in the Baltics had already isolated Army Group North on the Courland peninsula. In the south, below the Carpathian Mountains, other Red Army forces fought off efforts by General Otto Wöhler's Army Group South to break the Soviet ring around Budapest, then launched an advance toward Vienna and central Austria.

The Soviet infantry moved out three hours after the shelling began and almost immediately overran the dug-in defenders. By midday, Soviet tanks were rumbling through the German rear areas. Fifteen miles behind the front, they overran the Fourth Panzer Army's mobile reserves, two armored divisions from General Walther Nehring's XXIV Panzer Corps, before the German tanks could even deploy.

By the end of the second day, the First Ukrainian Front had advanced to depths of up to twenty-four miles on a front thirty-six miles wide. The Fourth Panzer Army had disintegrated. Remnants of its LXVIII Panzer Corps retreated southwestward toward Krakow to join the Seventeenth Army while Nehring's two shattered armored divisions staggered back to Kielce with stragglers from his infantry units. There, Nehring's men were joined by remnants of General Hermann Recknagel's battered XLII Corps.

The next day, January 14, Marshal Zhukov's First Belorussian Front blasted out of its bridgeheads at Magnuszew and Pulawy. General Smilo von Lüttwitz's Ninth Army was ready, alerted by the catastrophe unfolding on its right flank. But preparedness counted for little against the ferocity of the Soviet onslaught. At Magnuszew alone, in an area barely fifteen miles wide by seven deep, the Russians had amassed 400,000 men.

Like Konev, Zhukov began the attack with a massive artillery bombardment. His infantry and armor then smashed and scattered the two corps and part of a third that stood in the way. On the 15th, the Soviets seized Radom, the Ninth Army's main supply base, thirty-five miles west of Pulawy, while Zhukov's southern flank armies joined with Konev's northern flank armies and drove the survivors of Nehring's panzer and Recknagel's infantry corps out of the Kielce-Radom corridor.

Zhukov's northern flank armies, rolling forward with relentless weight, encircled Warsaw. The commandant of the German garrison in Warsaw ordered the city evacuated on the 17th. Soldiers of the Polish First Army assigned to the First Belorussian Front liberated their battle-scarred capital that same day. Meanwhile, to the south, the First Ukrainian Front was shattering everything in its path. Konev's spearheads had advanced 100 miles on a front that was 160 miles wide and crossed the Warta River. Krakow fell on January 19.

The supporting offensive on the northern flank did not fare as well. The bad weather that had aided Konev in southern Poland hindered General Chernyakovsky in northern East Prussia. When the Third Belorussian Front began its artillery bombardment on the morning of January 13, the Soviet gunners did not know that General Erhard Raus's Third Panzer Army had already abandoned its forward positions. When Chernyakovsky's forces attacked, they met resistance and managed only slight gains. The battle

Bundled against the bitter cold, German soldiers hitch horses to sleds in preparation for a retreat. By the middle of January 1945, Army Group A in central Poland was fighting desperately for its survival.

seesawed for several days, with towns changing hands several times before the Russians seized the important prize of Tilsit on January 18.

On Chernyakovsky's southern flank, General Rokossovsky also found the going tough. On January 14, the Second Belorussian Front broke out from its Narew River bridgeheads. But German resistance stiffened after Reinhardt committed Army Group Center's reserves, the 7th Panzer Division and the crack panzergrenadier division, Grossdeutschland.

Hitler mistakenly interpreted this temporary success to mean that the Soviet attack in East Prussia had been halted. Against Guderian's advice, the Führer stripped Reinhardt of Lieut. General Dietrich von Saucken's Panzer Corps Grossdeutschland, ordering the two-division force to help defend Kielce in Army Group A's sector, 100 miles south of Warsaw. But Kielce was already in Soviet hands.

Rokossovsky exploited this weakening in East Prussia by committing two tank corps to his assault force. Aided by a spell of clear weather that allowed Soviet warplanes to fly, the Second Belorussian Front regained its momentum. The German Second Army, reinforced by sailors from Baltic naval stations, Luftwaffe ground crews, and members of the Volkssturm, struggled to hold its ground. By the 18th, Rokossovsky had pressed forward forty miles on a seventy-mile-wide front. On the 21st, his forces swarmed into Tannenberg, site of Field Marshal Paul von Hindenburg's crushing victory over the Russians in 1914. The Germans hastily removed the remains of their great World War I hero and his wife from the mausoleum where they were buried and destroyed the memorial before they fled.

German civilians in the path of the Soviet advance now experienced the horrors of war in a way they had thus far been spared. When military commanders had sought permission to evacuate them before the onset of the offensive, Hitler rejected the requests as defeatist and, through his personal secretary, Martin Bormann, ordered local gauleiters to keep their subjects at home. The Soviet command, meanwhile, had promoted the theme of revenge in troop indoctrination meetings for months, reminding the Red Army of the outrages the German troops had committed against the Soviet population. Trapped between the intransigence of Hitler and the hatred of a vengeful enemy, German civilians died by the tens of thousands.

Anton Riess, the deputy mayor of a village in the Warta district of annexed Poland, was startled to find a German officer in a ditch near his house on the evening of January 18. When Riess asked him if he had come from the front, the officer snorted, "Front! Front! That's over. I'm the only one left from my company. The others are all gone. The whole regiment—all gone. I got into the woods and ran." The officer's next words sent a chill through Riess: "In a few hours, Ivan is going to get here."

Riess reported this information by telephone to the gauleiter of his district, but he received only a lecture in reply. The officer was a traitor who should be arrested, he was told; there was nothing to worry about. Riess was still on the phone when two fur-hatted men in gray-brown uniforms burst into the room. Before he could say another word, one shot him with a pistol. The Soviet soldiers then took his ring and watch and smashed the telephone. Outside, the sounds of gunfire and breaking doors and the first screams of women filled the air.

By the end of the invasion's first fortnight, the Soviet juggernaut had rumbled over much of Poland and substantial sections of East Prussia, the main exception being the area around Königsberg where remnants of Army Group Center stubbornly resisted. Isolated fortress towns such as Breslau and Poznan in western Poland were also holding out, but the German army groups had lost contact with each other as the Soviets, inspired by the promise of rewards for the first units to reach the Oder, raced westward at a pace of twelve to twenty miles a day. The number of German troops taken prisoner more than tripled from the first week of the offensive to the second, rising from 25,000 to 86,000. In some places, the Soviets struck so fast that there was no time to escape. When Russian tanks rolled onto the streets of Elbing near the Baltic Sea on the evening of January 23, shoppers were still in the stores, and smoke—not of battle but of industry—was rising from factory smokestacks.

Shortly after the offensive began, Guderian intensified his pleas for help. "The position of Army Group A has become acute," he wired Hitler on January 15. "The threat to the Upper Silesian industrial region is imminent." The Führer acknowledged the gravity of the situation mainly by moving his headquarters from the Adlerhorst to his bunker beneath the old Reich Chancellery in Berlin. He also ordered the western front forces to go on the defensive, but still offered only minimal reinforcements. Guderian was elated to hear that the Sixth SS Panzer Army, with its core of four SS panzer divisions, was being transferred from the western front, then learned to his dismay that the powerful force was going to Hungary, not Poland. When he protested to Hitler, he was treated to a lecture on the economic importance of the Hungarian oil fields, which Hitler regarded as the most strategically critical section of the entire eastern front.

Guderian again beseeched Hitler to move General Schörner's Army Group North from Courland to Poland, but the answer was still no. Instead of Schörner's thirty divisions, Hitler sent Schörner himself, a loyal National Socialist and one of the Führer's favorite generals, to replace Harpe as commander of Army Group A.

Hitler was by now detecting disobedience and disaffection daily. He exploded again on January 17 when he learned that Warsaw had been abandoned in defiance of his express order. "Now Hitler's rage knew no bounds," Guderian wrote in his memoirs. "He completely lost all comprehension of, and interest in, the frightful general situation and thought of nothing but the misfortune of losing Warsaw." The ensuing several days were devoted to identifying and punishing those responsible, with the witch hunt zeroing in on the general staff officers who had handled the orders dealing with the withdrawal. Guderian argued heatedly that as chief of staff he, not his subordinates, should be held accountable, but Hitler raged at the OKH staff officers he had long distrusted. It was "intolerable," he fumed, "that a group of intellectuals should presume to press their views on their superiors." He ordered three close aides of Guderian arrested and subjected Guderian himself to a time-consuming interrogation.

After the Warsaw crisis, Hitler severely restricted the authority of his field commanders. From that time on, every commander down to division level had to report every decision to attack, move troops, disengage, or surrender to the Führer's headquarters early enough so that Hitler could intervene if he saw fit. The commanders were to tell him nothing but the "unvarnished truth"; any deviation, deliberate or accidental, would be met with "draconian punishment."

One commander was contemplating direct disobedience at the exact moment that this order was promulgated. Army Group Center commander Hans Reinhardt, whose Fourth Army under General Friedrich Hossbach was encircled by the Soviets on a Narew River bend, had repeatedly sought permission to let Hossbach try a breakout, only to be refused each time. Reinhardt's chief of staff wrote in his journal that Hitler's replies were "quick, seldom to the point, and untroubled by understanding."

While Reinhardt wondered if he ought to disobey, Hossbach went ahead and did just that, sending his men through the wall of Red Army troops blocking the way to the Baltic coast. When Hitler realized what had happened, he accused Reinhardt and Hossbach of treason and dismissed them. On January 27, Hitler made General Lothar Rendulic, who had replaced Schörner as commander of German forces in Courland, the new leader of Army Group Center.

In late January, Hitler finally yielded to Guderian's appeals: He ordered five divisions from Courland and several more from the west to bolster the front between the Vistula and Oder rivers. Among them was the 21st Panzer Division, which included Colonel Hans von Luck's 125th Regiment. Luck's troops were battle-hardened veterans who had been in combat since D-day. He spoke briefly to them before they entrained. He wanted them to understand exactly what they were fighting for now—when the war was all but lost. Luck explained that they were going to the old fortress of Küstrin on the Oder, forty miles east of Berlin and directly in the path of the onrushing Soviets. "It will be our last battle," Luck told his men. "Forget all the slogans about a 'Thousand-Year Reich' and 'the final victory that must be ours.' From now on, we are fighting solely for survival, for our homeland, our wives, mothers, and children, whom we want to save from a fate none of us can imagine."

By the time Luck's regiment reached its new post, Zhukov's First Belorussian Front was across the Oder north of Küstrin and also at Frankfurt an der Oder, eighteen miles to the south. Farther south, Konev's First Ukrainian Front was sweeping through the Reich's last large industrial centers in Upper Silesia, deliberately leaving a path of retreat open so that

Soviet troops from the First Ukrainian Front overrun Gleiwitz, an industrial city in Upper Silesia (present-day Poland) in January 1945. Relatively untouched by Allied bombing, the region's factories were still running when the Russians arrived as the Germans tried to squeeze out the last possible production.

the Seventeenth Army could escape, thus forestalling a clash of arms that might cause the destruction of the valuable mines and factories. On their approach to Silesia, Konev's troops discovered and liberated the infamous death camp at Auschwitz.

On the northern end of the battle zone, the Third Belorussian Front reached the Baltic Sea at the end of January and sealed off Königsberg. The withdrawal of Hossbach's Fourth Army had left most portions of East Prussia unprotected. The Third Panzer Army was completely broken; some units regrouped on the Samland peninsula, west of Königsberg. Others retreated into the city itself. To the southwest, the Soviets bypassed and surrounded the fortress city of Poznan, which was held by 10,000 troops, including 2,000 cadets from the local military academy.

By the first week of February, the First Ukrainian and First Belorussian fronts had advanced some 250 miles and established a line that zigzagged for 300 miles along the Oder. In the Baltic region, the Third Belorussian Front had overrun most of East Prussia, while the Second Belorussian Front had reached the area just south of West Prussia.

On January 26, Hitler decided to create a new army group in the east and to rename the other eastern-front commands. The new Army Group Vistula, fashioned from the Second, Ninth, and Third Panzer armies, plus battalions of Volkssturm, would confront the Soviets driving for Berlin and

During a pause in their retreat, crewmen of a Sturmgeschütz assault gun share a hot drink with two panzergrenadiers dressed in snow camouflage. The latter wear color-coded armbands to distinguish themselves from the Russians, who wore similar winter uniforms.

northern Germany. Rendulic's Army Group Center became Army Group North, and Schörner's Army Group A became Army Group Center. More important than the name changes, however, was the man the Führer chose to lead the new command—Heinrich Himmler.

The choice appalled Guderian who derided Himmler as a military ignoramus. "I used such argumentative powers as I possessed," Guderian later wrote, "in an attempt to stop such an idiocy being perpetrated on the unfortunate eastern front." Besides Himmler's lack of military experience, he had too many other jobs, including running the SS, the Reserve Army, and training the Volkssturm.

In late January, Himmler rode his private train to Army Group Vistula's headquarters at Deutsch Krone, sixty miles north of Poznan. Lacking a staff and adequate communications facilities, he had the near-impossible task of holding what remained of the German line in the northern sector of the front while blocking the Soviets from moving into Pomerania and West Prussia. Himmler's first moves were not encouraging. He ordered the evacuation of several small fortress towns, resulting in the loss of several bridgeheads that would have been valuable for launching counteroffensives. Then he ordered the relief of a town allegedly in Soviet hands—only there were no Soviets there.

Guderian, in the meantime, was edging ever closer to the fire in his relationship with Hitler. Convinced that Germany's best hope lay in negotiating an armistice with Britain and the United States while continuing the fight against the Soviet Union, Guderian proposed to Foreign Minister Joachim von Ribbentrop that the two of them broach the idea with Hitler. Ribbentrop declined.

Early in February, Guderian urged Hitler to withdraw forces from Courland, Italy, Norway, and the Balkans to support a last-ditch offensive in the east. "It is not just pigheadedness on my part," he argued. "I assure you I am acting solely in Germany's interests." Hitler leaped to his feet, trembling with rage. "How dare you speak to me like that!" he shouted. "Don't you think I am fighting for Germany? My whole life has been one long struggle for Germany." The confrontation ended only when Hermann Göring took Guderian by the arm and eased him out of the room.

Meanwhile, civilians trapped in Königsberg endured artillery bombardments, air raids, rumors, shortages, and rare interludes of peace. Dr. Hans von Lehndorff, a surgeon who was working in an army hospital in the city, kept a journal during the siege. He wrote of residents discussing cyanide "in a casual, nonchalant way, as people might talk about food." He saw German soldiers retreating, firing as they went, while women swept the doorways of houses nearby. "Mortars rattle like the wheel of fortune at the country fair," he wrote, "but it is still difficult to grasp the harsh reality."

At the end of the first week of February, the Soviet pressure eased slightly. A thaw turned the roads to mush and made the long-distance Soviet supply runs more difficult; the spearheads of both the Konev and Zhukov fronts were now 300 miles ahead of their depots. The Oder line was calm as Zhukov issued orders to consolidate gains and stockpile fuel and ammunition. Himmler wrote Guderian that the change in the weather was a "gift of fate." General Schörner pulled back his rechristened Army Group Center to a momentarily quiet front extending 300 miles from the Carpathian Mountains to the Neisse and Oder rivers. Himmler was trying to find the muscle for a counterattack.

Around Poznan, however, the Soviet vise tightened. On the night of February 16, part of the small garrison broke out, slipping single file through the enemy lines. After holding out for five more days, the officer in charge of the city's defenses, a Major Gonell, asked Himmler for permission to break out with the men remaining. Receiving no reply, Gonell called his officers together and informed them that each man was free to try to escape on his own. He then retired to his quarters, lay down on a swastika battle flag, and shot himself.

The thaw and the overextended Soviet supply lines also helped the Germans in the northern sector of the front. One of the Third Army corps, renamed Army Detachment Samland, broke the Soviet ring around Königsberg, opening a narrow lifeline to the Samland peninsula. The Second Army stalled the Second Belorussian Front in Pomerania, and a thrust by the Ninth Army, with Colonel von Luck's 125th Regiment in the vanguard, opened a corridor to the besieged garrison in Küstrin. Luck's men went into battle as soon as they got off the train that had brought them east. The troops were thrilled to see Luftwaffe Stukas supporting them—the first friendly aircraft they had sighted in months.

Farther south, however, Konev's First Ukrainian Front kept the Soviet drive moving. Bursting out of a bridgehead at Steinau, five of Konev's armies surrounded Breslau, with its 35,000-man garrison and 116,000 civilian inhabitants. Four days later, the Soviets trapped nearly 12,000 soldiers and civilians at Glogau and pressed on to the Neisse River. But Konev too was running short of supplies; he halted his campaign at the Brandenburg border in late February.

The great exodus of civilians from East Prussia, Silesia, and elsewhere was now in full flood. Fleeing with whatever they could carry on their backs or in farm carts and baby carriages, the shuffling, ill-clad, freezing refugees—1945 was one of the coldest winters on record—clogged the snow-bordered roads. In East Prussia alone, more than half of the 2.3 million

A column of Soviet self-propelled assault guns roll through an East Prussian town, heading toward the Frisches Haff. Amid the flotsam left behind are several German dead, including one soldier whose body has been ground beneath the tracks of the westward-moving Russian tanks.

population had fled their homes by mid-February. They crossed the long sandspit called Frische Nehrung west of Königsberg and trudged over the ice-covered Vistula delta to Danzig. In the port of Pillau at the southern tip of the Samland peninsula, they jammed the docks and clamored to be allowed on the evacuation ships that were queuing up in the harbor. Russian planes sometimes strafed the shambling columns, and on at least one occasion, Soviet tanks crushed a band of civilians under their tracks. Thousands more died of exposure, perished from disease, or fell into the icy waters and drowned.

A German army doctor traveling in the Vistula Valley saw endless lines of refugees trudging through the snow and mud. "Their columns barely inched along," he wrote. "Many had potato sacks pulled over their heads with holes cut out for their eyes." In the open wagons, children, the elderly, and the sick "lay deep in the snow-wet straw or under wet, soiled feather

German refugees flee over the treacherous ice of the partially frozen Frisches Haff, a six-to-eleven-mile-wide lagoon separating the East Prussian mainland from the Gulf of Danzig. Many refugees perished before they could reach evacuation ships waiting in the Baltic.

beds. The treks were strangely silent. The hoofs of the horses thumped on the snow, and here and there a wheel creaked. The roads were so congested that for a time we tried to make headway across the country and along field paths. But even there, refugee treks blocked the way—an indescribable, ghostly procession with eyes full of misery and wretchedness, quiet resignation, and a helpless plaint beyond words."

A young woman who fled Breslau shortly before it was surrounded chronicled her ordeal in a letter to her mother. Carrying only her infant daughter, milk, and blankets, she joined a caravan of "thousands and thousands of women." They hiked almost ten miles to the town of Kanth, where, she wrote, "I saw the first dead children, in the ditches and even on the square. I knocked at houses because I thought I would find someone who would let me warm the milk for Gabi, but I had no luck. It was terribly cold, the wind was like ice, snow was falling, and we had nothing warm to eat. I tried to give Gabi the breast, but she did not take it because everything was so cold."

When the young woman finally found refuge at a farmhouse and removed the baby's blankets, the child was dead. "I wrapped her up well and put her deep in the snow beside the road," the letter continued. "I couldn't carry her anymore. Gabi won't be alone there, because thousands of women with their children were with me, and they all put their dead in the ditches by the roadside. You know, she was only four months old."

The tales of murder, rape, and horror that set German civilians to flight were not rumors but chilling fact. Red Army soldiers had been told that they were not liable for civil crimes on German territory and that German property was theirs by right. Leaflets dropped to the troops bore a chilling message from writer-propagandist Ilya Ehrenburg, exhorting them: "Kill the Germans. Kill all Germans." The enemy was not just the army but the entire German nation. The Soviets burned villages, butchered town officials, and hunted down clergymen and landowners. In the worst instances, they mutilated their victims or dragged them to death behind horses. They raped and brutalized women of all ages.

At Danzig, Pillau, and other ports, the atmosphere was a bedlam born of desperation. In Pillau, a short-lived order allowed no one to board evacuation ships except parents or grandparents carrying children. A few who got aboard tried to throw their small children to frantic relatives or friends on the pier. Some infants dropped into the water, others were caught and used by strangers. Squeezing onto a vessel was still no guarantee of safety. Thousands died when Allied planes and submarines attacked several of the ships.

Even the Nazi officials charged with enforcing Martin Bormann's fiat barring civilians from fleeing joined the flight. Erich Koch, the gauleiter of East Prussia who had punished hundreds for desertion, escaped to Denmark on a chartered icebreaker carrying his car, trunks, staff, bodyguard, and pet greyhounds. Albert Forster, the Danzig-West Prussia district chief, sailed away on a yacht.

The Soviet atrocities only subsided when Stalin issued a secret order to his top commanders declaring that violence directed at civilians was "unwise" in that it was "likely to increase the enemy's resistance and delay termination of the war." By that time, the vengeful damage, of course, had already been done, and the bitter enmity between Germany and Russia had attained a new intensity.

Guderian, studying the situation maps in February, noticed that the armies of Zhukov's First Belorussian Front had raced ahead of the other Soviet forces and now occupied a salient with its tip on the Oder and its

A German woman wanders through the flaming streets of Breslau searching for shelter. The city's defense forces inflicted nearly 60,000 casualties on the Soviets and succeeded in holding out until May 6, 1945.

northern and southern flanks exposed. He suggested a quick two-pronged attack on the flanks before the other Soviet armies closed up. Hitler opted instead for a single thrust from the north, starting from Stargard in Pomerania, in an offensive code-named *Sonnenwende* (Solstice). OKH began to scrape together troops. The plan was to strike with three attack groups on a thirty-mile-wide front. The primary unanswered question was who would lead the attack.

The Sonnenwende battle zone was in the sector of Himmler's Army Group Vistula, but Guderian was unwilling to trust the assignment to the militarily unskilled SS leader. He wanted his chief deputy, General Walther Wenck, to lead the operation. Intelligence reports estimated that the Russians had the capacity to increase their strength on the Oder by four divisions a day, so there was no time to lose. The stage was set for another showdown with Hitler. It came on February 13.

The first issue was timing. Hitler and Himmler proposed a delay until more fuel and ammunition were available. Guderian insisted that they could not afford to wait. "I don't permit you to accuse me of wanting to wait," Hitler shouted. Guderian, with Himmler only a few feet away, then demanded that Wenck be placed in charge "since otherwise there can be no prospect of the attack succeeding." Guderian's remark enraged Hitler. "The Reichsführer is man enough to carry out the attack," he screamed. Guderian retorted that Himmler lacked both the experience and the staff to lead the offensive.

Hitler's cheeks flushed. He clenched his fists and paced angrily, the veins on his head standing out sharply. "I don't permit you to tell me that the Reichsführer is incapable of performing his duties," he raved. Guderian struggled to remain calm as the Führer screamed in his face. Hitler fulminated for two full hours—aides said afterward that they had never seen him so angry—but Guderian held his ground. Suddenly, Hitler stopped in front of Himmler and announced, "Well, Himmler, General Wenck will arrive at your headquarters tonight and will take charge of the attack." Hitler then sat down and smiled at Guderian. "The general staff has won a battle this day," he said.

Wenck and Himmler had a chilly meeting the next day at Himmler's new headquarters at Prenzlau, thirty miles in the rear of the Oder front. The Reichsführer, still living comfortably for a front-line commander, then retreated to a nearby clinic to rest. His main contribution to the attack that began on February 15 was a witless exhortation to his men from his bed: "Forward through the mud! Forward through the snow! Forward by day! Forward by night! Forward for the liberation of German soil!"

Bringing together the large force needed for Operation Sonnenwende was too great a task for Germany's crippled railroads. The day before the attack, scarcely half of Wenck's troops had arrived, and those of them who were present lacked ammunition, gasoline, and supplies. Realizing that a small attack was better than none, Wenck launched the operation anyway, sending the newly created Eleventh SS Panzer Army south to rescue a small garrison that had been cut off at Arnswalde. By early afternoon, the Germans had liberated their comrades and seized the nearby town of Pyritz as well. The following day, Wenck threw more divisions into the battle, but with only light air and artillery support, the Germans gained little ground. Then, rainy weather turned the landscape into mud, confining the panzers to the roads and limiting their effectiveness. But the most serious blow fell on the night of February 17 when Wenck was returning from a conference in Berlin. While relieving the exhausted driver of his staff car, Wenck fell asleep at the wheel and smashed into a bridge parapet, suffering injuries serious enough to require hospitalization. Sonnenwende sputtered forward for two more days before Himmler emerged from his bed to issue a directive for "regrouping."

Zhukov, who had been biding his time, counterattacked in strength on February 19, retaking the town of Arnswalde and driving north to within twelve miles of Stettin, which lay beyond Stargard on the lower Oder River. Two days later, Hitler called off Sonnenwende and transferred three of Army Group Vistula's divisions to Schörner's Army Group Center.

Himmler's army group had suffered heavy casualties in a battle that had yielded no territory or tactical advantage. For the Germans, the only plus was psychological: Stavka, more alarmed than it should have been by the ill-starred attack, decided to postpone the final push to Berlin. With Konev halted on the Neisse at the Brandenburg frontier, Zhukov took the First Belorussian Front north, away from the high road to the German capital, while Rokossovsky's Second Belorussian Front drove on Danzig.

Throughout the battles on the eastern front, Hitler's attention had rarely strayed long from Hungary, the source of three-fourths of the Reich's remaining supply of oil. In early March, he launched an offensive, opti-

mistically called *Fruhlingserwachen*, or Spring Awakening, to gain some space between the Soviets and the Nagykanizsa oil fields, southwest of Budapest, and to retake the Hungarian capital itself, which had fallen the previous month. The battle raged for weeks between General Wöhler's Army Group South and the Second and Third Ukrainian fronts. By April 2, the Russians had crushed the German force and seized the oil fields. Eleven days later, they seized Vienna.

Meanwhile, Stavka's decision to halt the drive on Berlin in late February had caught Guderian by surprise. He was more puzzled when Zhukov's powerful First Belorussian Front swung north toward the Baltic in early March. Zhukov aimed for the city of Kolberg, 125 miles west of Danzig. At the same time, Rokossovsky's Second Belorussian Front attempted to reach the coast at a point that would separate the Second Panzer Army, clinging to West Prussia, from the Third Panzer Army on its right.

Kolberg was a symbol of heroic resistance to the German people. The coastal fortress had withstood the Russians during Frederick the Great's Seven Years' War and had bravely resisted Napoleon in 1807; Joseph Goebbels's propaganda ministry had only recently released a film celebrating the event. When Zhukov's forces reached the coast and isolated the famous fortress on March 4, Kolberg was under siege again. Zhukov captured Stargard on the same day, while Rokossovsky's armies battered their way toward the Gulf of Danzig.

Hitler demanded a counterattack. Lieut. General Eberhard Kinzel, who had replaced Raus as commander of the Third Panzer Army, replied via Guderian's deputy that the Führer was fighting the war "on paper." A counterattack was out of the question; now even lower-ranking generals were daring to talk back.

Kinzel pulled his army back to a precarious bridgehead at Stettin near the Oder estuary, but the Germans soon had to evacuate that position as well. Rokossovsky broke through to the coast northwest of Danzig on March 12. Six days afterward, the garrison at Kolberg capitulated, but not before 80,000 residents and refugees had escaped by sea behind a screen of Volkssturm troops.

Meanwhile, Colonel Hans von Luck's regiment, which had arrived in February from the western front, had moved from the Küstrin area to Lower Silesia and attached to General Schörner's Army Group Center. It was at this time that Luck had his first exposure to the recently instituted "flying" drumhead courts-martial, which gave roving officers the authority to summarily execute soldiers accused of disobedience, malingering, or desertion. Luck had sent a soldier to the rear to bring up some newly repaired half-tracks. After making the arrangements, the sergeant was eating dinner at an inn when a judge advocate general spotted him, charged him with desertion, and had him shot. When Luck called headquarters to protest, he was informed that his superiors endorsed the punishment. To Luck, it was another sign of bankrupt leadership. "This war was no longer to be won with flying drumhead courts-martial," he wrote later. "The endless slogans and proclamations sounded to us at the front like sheer mockery."

Shortly afterward, Luck's regiment took part in a surprise attack on a rail link at Luban, fifty miles east of Dresden. The attack succeeded in taking the rail junction and recapturing several villages in a week of heavy fighting. It also gave Luck his first glimpse of Russian revenge: brutalized women "screaming or completely apathetic," plundered homes, and civilian dead.

Himmler's brief tenure as an army group commander on the eastern front ended in March at Guderian's instigation. After not hearing from Himmler for several days, Guderian went looking for him. He was surprised to find him at his clinic retreat. Guderian, whose diplomatic skills were improving by necessity, delicately pointed out that a man with so many other jobs perhaps ought to relinquish one of them. When Himmler replied that the Führer would never agree, Guderian offered to make the case personally. To his surprise, the Führer approved on March 20. When Himmler's replacement, General Gotthard Heinrici, showed up at Army Group Vistula headquarters two days later, Himmler greeted him with a rambling discourse on his achievements. A telephone call finally silenced him—it was one of his generals reporting another Russian breakthrough. Himmler handed the receiver to Heinrici. "You command the army group now," he said. "Please give the appropriate order."

The Soviets next fixed their sights on clearing the Upper Silesian industrial region. The German assault at Luban had kept the rail line open between the Silesian factories and Berlin, but most of the German units that remained behind were stitched together from the remnants of shattered divisions, Volkssturm troops, and walking wounded. Konev's First Ukrainian Front attacked on March 15. His armies rolled southwest on either side of Oppeln, and from north of Ratibor, advancing slowly at first but gaining speed on the 17th when the two segments of the offensive came together in a ring around the LVI Panzer Corps. The panzers broke out three days later, but Konev kept the pressure on until Schörner withdrew his last units from Ratibor on the 30th. Upper Silesia, with the exception of the fortress city of Breslau, now belonged to the Soviets.

The Red Army march through densely populated Silesia precipitated an even greater civilian exodus than the sweep through East Prussia: In early 1944, the German population in Silesia had stood at 4.7 million; in April 1945, it was 620,000. Breslau, the gritty exception, held out until the end of

General Gotthard Heinrici, who replaced Heinrich Himmler as commander of Army Group Vistula on March 20, 1945, inspects one of his units. Forty days later, he was dismissed for pulling back his troops rather than sacrificing them in an attempt to hold the line north of Berlin.

the war with a hodgepodge garrison of policemen, airmen, military school students, one newly raised army division, and Volkssturm members.

Knowing that Zhukov's armies on the Oder remained the most serious threat to Berlin, Hitler issued an order in mid-March directing the Ninth Army, of Heinrici's Army Group Vistula, to drive the Soviets from their bridgehead near Küstrin. On March 22, Zhukov's First Belorussian Front struck before the Germans could get their forces organized, and once again Küstrin was encircled. When a counterattack failed two days later, General Theodor Busse, commander of the Ninth Army, and Heinrici decided to forego another try. Hitler, however, demanded a second attempt. But it too fell short. On March 29, Russian infantry stormed the castlelike Küstrin fortress. The garrison commander ordered a breakout and escaped with the few men he had left.

The Küstrin battle proved to be the last for Guderian as chief of the general staff. Hitler had excoriated Busse at a meeting on March 27 for employing too weak an artillery bombardment against Zhukov's forces.

Guderian defended his general by pointing out that Busse had only a limited amount of ammunition. The argument continued the next day. When Guderian again disputed Hitler, the Führer damned the general staff and the entire officer corps. "It seemed as if he were about to hurl himself at Guderian," one witness wrote. "For seconds there was a deadly hush broken only by heavy breathing." Then it was Guderian's turn to explode. He reviled Hitler's generalship, condemned his failure to end the Ardennes offensive sooner, and accused him of deserting the people of eastern Germany. Hitler suddenly asked everyone but Guderian and the OKW chief, Field Marshal Wilhelm Keitel, to leave the room. Hitler then quietly announced that Guderian's health required him to take an immediate six-week convalescent leave. Guderian assented.

Danzig fell on March 30, yielding 10,000 prisoners, 140 tanks, and forty-five U-boats. The outposts of resistance east of the Oder could now be counted on the fingers of one hand: Breslau, the Courland peninsula, the Vistula delta east of Danzig, and Königsberg.

The 100,000 civilians in Königsberg knew that time was running out. By late March, Soviet armies were moving on the city from the east, south, and southwest. Loudspeakers blared from low-flying aircraft: "You men of the Volkssturm, go home! We won't harm you old granddaddies. Throw those rifles away." The mood among civilians shifted from pessimism to fatalism. Dr. von Lehndorff, who was chronicling life in the city while working as a surgeon in an army hospital, detected a "definite feeling of approaching the end." During a visit to another hospital, he found a picture of Winston Churchill displayed in the doctors' dining room and learned that the doctors were studying Russian.

"Very early in the morning of April 3, I began to feel uncomfortable in my room on the second floor because heavier shelling was going on," he wrote in his journal. "I took almost all my belongings downstairs. An hour later, just as we were operating, a load of small bombs rattled on top of us. I ran out in the yard and saw a big hole in the second floor. The only bomb that hit had gone into my window." Two days later, there was a daylong bombing raid on the city "with no sign of defense." The city center was covered by a "black cloud like a mountain range out of which flames were shooting." Lehndorff slept fitfully, dreaming that he was sitting in a sylvan cottage watching hordes of torchbearing Russians "with strange, wild faces" glide toward him.

General Alexander Vasilevsky, the new commander of the Third Belorussian Front besieging Königsberg, had decided to throw against the city everything he had—137,000 men, 2,400 planes, hundreds of tanks, and the multiple rocket launchers that the Germans called "Stalin's organs." Va-

A bicyclist approaches an abandoned German armored personnel carrier on a rubble-filled street in Königsberg after Lieut. General Otto Lasch *(inset)* surrendered the city on April 9, 1945, in a effort to avoid further bloodshed. Infuriated by the unauthorized capitulation, Hitler ordered the general condemned to death and his family thrown into a concentration camp.

silevsky's intricate preparations included construction of a model of Königsberg showing its forts and strongpoints at a scale of 1 to 3,000. Soviet spies in civilian clothes and German uniforms infiltrated the town. The German garrison commander, Lieut. General Otto Lasch, had 35,000 troops manning a defensive network of pillboxes, fortified buildings, and strongpoints, but he knew it was nowhere near enough. His superior, Fourth Army commander Lieut. General Friedrich Müller, who had replaced Hossbach, threatened to report him for pessimism.

On April 6, the Soviets struck at eight different points on the Königsberg perimeter. Blockading some forts and destroying others, they smashed their way into the city by nightfall. Lasch asked permission to evacuate as many troops and civilians as he could to the Samland peninsula and Pillau, but Müller refused. The next day, the Russians cut the lifeline to Pillau. Good weather on April 7 allowed the Soviet air force to drop 550 tons of bombs while the infantry advanced in fierce house-to-house fighting.

Small groups of Germans tried to break through the encirclement. One detachment of panzergrenadiers spent the night of April 8 in a cemetery, but they were spotted moving across a dam at dawn the next morning. "All hell was let loose in no time at all," a major who was with them wrote. The Germans hid in a marsh all day, watching the city "veiled in smoke and fire into which the heavy guns tore fresh wounds time and again."

Inside Königsberg, Lasch broadcast his final message on the afternoon of April 9: "Ammunition gone, stores destroyed." Although isolated pockets of Germans fought to the death, the garrison commander made contact with the Soviets that evening and signed a surrender document on the 10th, with Russian cameramen recording the moment on film. When Hitler learned of the unauthorized surrender, he condemned Lasch to death and ordered his family arrested, including a son-in-law who commanded a battalion; Hitler also relieved Müller of his command.

The Russians swept onto the Frische Nehrung and trained their guns on Pillau, the last German stronghold in East Prussia. Wehrmacht forces stubbornly held out for six days before finally capitulating on April 25. In all, 42,000 German soldiers died in the Königsberg area, and another 92,000 were taken prisoner. One-fourth of the city's civilian population—25,000 people—also lost their lives.

Dr. von Lehndorff could only watch helplessly as Red Army troops barged into his hospital. They robbed first. "My fountain pen vanished," Lehndorff recalled. "Money and papers flew all over the place." Then the teenage soldiers began to rape the nurses, "flinging themselves like wolves on the women." Lehndorff despaired of describing the appalling cruelty he witnessed. "I felt guilty," he wrote, "that I was still alive."

On April 6, when General Rendulic, now head of Army Group Courland, reported to Hitler for his next assignment, he was struck by the decline in the Führer's appearance. Two weeks away from his fifty-sixth birthday, Hitler was a bent and stooped old man. He dragged his left leg and cradled his left arm with his right hand. But as another general who saw him the same day reported, the Führer had lost none of his zealotry. When General Heinrici warned that Army Group Vistula might be overwhelmed by the huge numbers of Russians opposing it, Hitler replied: "I always hear figures. I hear nothing about the inner strength of the troops. If your soldiers are filled with fanatical faith, they will win this battle."

On April 15, the eve of the final Soviet drive on Berlin, Hitler issued an order promising the arrival of units that did not exist and implored his

The Final Days of an Elite Division

In the early spring of 1945, the fate of the Grossdeutschland Division was sealed. The proud 21,000-man unit, which had fought with distinction at Kharkov and Kursk and carried the title "Bodyguard of the German People," had been reduced to a mere 4,000 men, trapped by the Red Army between the East Prussian city of Heiligenbeil and the Frisches Haff, the coastal inlet of the Gulf of Danzig.

"On March 24, the Russians attacked Heiligenbeil," recalled Sergeant Willibald Casper. "I remember the day well. It was my thirtieth birthday. I had a party in hell." Two days later, Adolf Hitler sanctioned the division's withdrawal to Pillau at the tip of the Samland peninsula. To get there, the weary veterans sailed across the Frisches Haff on a fleet of rafts and barges.

But Pillau was no haven. Shortly afterward, nearby Königsberg fell, allowing the Russians to transfer their strength to the Samland. On April 25, they drove the remnants of the Grossdeutschland onto the Frische Nehrung, the narrow sandspit separating the Gulf of Danzig from the Frisches Haff. From there, the survivors dispersed, some escaping to the west on evacuation ships. No more than 800 of them made it back to Germany where they surrendered to the Americans and British—only to be handed over to the Soviets in accordance with an Allied agreement to return German prisoners to the forces they had fought against.

Grossdeutschland troops cling to cliffs overlooking the Frisches Haff. "Many threw together rafts made from planks and watertight containers," Sergeant Casper explained later. "But most were flimsy, and at night we heard the cries of the drowning."

Major General Karl Lorenz (*right*), the commander of the Grossdeutschland Division, gives instructions for ferrying men across the Frisches Haff on March 27, 1945. The crossings took place at night to elude Russian artillery and aircraft.

Haggard soldiers disembark from a barge at Pillau. The Germans were forced to leave their tanks, assault guns, and heavy equipment on the other side of the Frisches Haff.

An officer in Pillau displays a sign instructing newly arrived troops to meet at gathering points named after German streets. Of his last days on the Samland peninsula, one soldier said: "Every moment we were looking death in the face."

soldiers to fight for their homes and families. "Bolshevism will suffer Asia's old fate," he declared. "It will founder on the capital of the German Reich."

Soviet strategy, coordinated by Zhukov, had been refined at Stavka meetings in Moscow in early April. Part of the plan called for encircling Berlin. The First Belorussian Front, now commanded by General Vasily D. Sokolovsky, was to thrust westward from Küstrin on a twenty-mile-wide front with the goal of reaching Berlin and the Elbe in fifteen days. Konev's First Ukrainian Front would advance west and northwest from their more southerly jumping-off point on the Neisse and move through Dresden toward the Elbe. Four days after the start of these attacks, the Second Belorussian Front would push northwest from the Stettin area to clear Pomerania and reach the remaining Baltic ports before the western Allies.

Again, the Soviet advantage in manpower and arms was enormous: The

Armored personnel carriers full of panzergrenadiers of the Third Panzer Army pass German infantrymen on the retreat to Stettin, a Baltic port eighty miles northeast of Berlin. There, they secured the bridges over the Oder and established a fifty-mile-wide bridgehead as an escape route for refugees and troops pouring into north-central Germany from the east.

three fronts totaled 2.5 million against roughly 250,000 Germans. Berlin's primary defenders were Army Group Vistula's Ninth Army under General Busse and the Third Panzer Army now under General Hasso-Eccard von Manteuffel. These forces held a line along the Oder from the Baltic Sea to the Neisse River. Busse defended the front directly east of Berlin while Manteuffel defended the northern approach. Busse had fourteen divisions with 512 tanks and assault guns and about 700 artillery pieces to pit against the First Belorussian Front's eighty-five divisions, 300 tanks and assault guns, and 17,000 pieces of artillery.

Hitler, inexplicably assuming that the final Soviet assault would come from Austria, sent three of Army Group Vistula's panzer divisions south. In addition, he took the precaution of naming commanders in chief for both north and south Germany—Grand Admiral Karl Dönitz in the north and Field Marshal Albert Kesselring in the south—in the event that the enemy cut the country in two.

The Soviet preparations included the construction of twenty-five bridges and the installation of 143 searchlights spaced 500 yards apart along the invasion front. The beams, trained at ground level, would supposedly blind the defenders during the predawn attack. Artillerymen practiced night firing to improve their precision on a battlefield where the front lines would be unusually close together.

Late on April 15, the Germans strengthened their main defensive line on the Seelow Heights five miles behind the forward positions at Küstrin. The Russians checked their weapons and listened to fiery speeches by their political officers. A thunderous artillery bombardment announced the start of the battle at 5:00 a.m. Twenty minutes later, the searchlights flicked on, and the infantry charged. The lights proved more of a hindrance than a help—in the smoke and dust, the beams created only a blinding glare. Worse, they silhouetted the attacking troops for the German gunners. Under heavy fire, the first wave bogged down in marshy terrain well short of the Seelow Heights.

The Russians got an inkling of the bitter struggle ahead from the Germans captured in the first assault: The prisoners claimed that German officers had orders to shoot anyone who attempted to retreat. Makeshift divisions composed of Luftwaffe personnel, Volkssturm, and Hitler Youth withstood the Red Army rush and held the Seelow Heights until the second day.

Konev's First Ukrainian Front had an easier time. Three armies crossed the Neisse between Forst and Muskau and quickly cut a six-mile-wide swath in the German lines. On April 18, the Soviets reached the outskirts of Cottbus and Spremberg, seventy and ninety miles southeast of Berlin, punching a hole between Schörner's Army Group Center and Heinrici's Army Group Vistula. Hans von Luck, now commanding a combat group, participated in the assault near Cottbus. His troops were battered, but when Luck ordered them to fall back, he received an angry call from his commanding general. "You have to fight where you are put," the general insisted. Luck was no longer willing to accept fanatical orders and said so. By the next day, his combat group and the bulk of the Ninth Army were nearly surrounded. Luck himself was taken prisoner.

Konev's First Ukrainian Front now swung north to support Sokolovsky's struggling First Belorussian Front. In the bunker beneath the Reich Chancellery, the atmosphere was cautiously optimistic: Field Marshal Keitel's rule of thumb declared that offensives collapsed if they failed to break through by the third day.

The breakthrough took place instead on the fourth and fifth days. Sokolovsky's tank armies broke out into open country west of the Seelow Heights on April 19, driving a wedge between Berlin and the Ninth Army. That same day, the First Ukrainian Front clattered to within ten miles of OKH headquarters at Zossen, fifteen miles south of Berlin. On April 20, Hitler's birthday, the Second Belorussian Front launched its attack from Stettin. Berlin was now within artillery range. The next day, armored troops from the First Ukrainian Front captured the Zossen complex with its network of underground offices and galleries. Teletypewriters were still clicking and telephones ringing; a German engineer obligingly took the occupiers on a tour of the communications facility. On the 22d, Konev's men seized the largest remaining German ammunition dump, at Jüterbog.

By now the orders from Hitler's bunker had degenerated into fantastic commands to nonexistent armies. The pieces on the battle maps represented sundered units devoid of fuel, ammunition, and the will to continue. From the bunker, a successful delaying action looked like a great victory. A small force north of Berlin, led by SS General Felix Steiner, was instructed to pierce Russian lines and break through to the city. Another order went out to General Walther Wenck's newly created Twelfth Army on the western front directing him to make an about-face and strike east to meet the Russians. Both orders were impossible to obey.

The Russians moved steadily to close the circle around Berlin. They advanced to Potsdam to the southwest, Bernau to the northeast, and Oranienburg to the north. On April 25, the First Belorussian and First Ukrainian fronts met northwest of Potsdam to connect the links southwest of Berlin. Soldiers from nine Soviet armies now manned the tightening noose around the dying capital.

Shortly after the Soviet offensive began, the American, British, and Canadian armies under General Dwight D. Eisenhower resumed their efforts to penetrate Germany from the west. Their planned January offensive had been delayed by Hitler's desperate gamble in the Ardennes, but in February the western Allies launched a major assault against the Rhine River, the last significant barrier shielding Germany in the west. The force Eisenhower had assembled included eighty-five full-strength divisions, with new divisions arriving from the United States at the rate of one per week. His plan was to make the initial strike toward the lower Rhine in northwestern Germany and to follow that thrust with an attack aimed at the middle Rhine Valley and the Ruhr, where Field Marshal Walther Model's Army Group B was deployed. Field Marshal Rundstedt opposed Eisenhower with seventy-three divisions operating at less than 40 percent of full strength.

The first phase of the Allied offensive was an assault by Field Marshal Sir Bernard Law Montgomery's British and Canadian troops on the Reichswald, a dense pine forest across the German border from Nijmegen, Holland. The Germans had built strong defensive positions along the northernmost sector of the West Wall, consisting of staggered lines of trenches, antitank ditches, fortified strongpoints, and command bunkers. The forest occupied a slender neck of land between the Maas and the Rhine rivers,

The Collapse of the Western Front

NORTH SEA

Zuider Zee

Amsterdam

NETHERLANDS

The Hague

Lek
Rotterdam

Antwerp

BELGIUM

FRANCE

Arnhem   Ijssel R.
TWENTY-FIFTH   River
Nijmegen   Cleves
Waal   CANADIAN FIRST
Maas River   Goch
21   Wesel
BRITISH SECOND
Roer River   US NINTH
Duisburg   Essen
Meuse   US NINTH
Jülich   Düsseldorf
Cologne   FIFTH
US FIRST   Bonn   Oberkassel
12   Remagen
US THIRD   Koblenz
LUXEMBOURG   Moselle
Redingen   River   River
Oppenheim
Saarbrücken   Mainz
US SEVENTH   US SEVENTH
Mannheim
Heidelberg

Rheine   FIRST (PART)
Ems   River   Munster   OB WEST
Lippe   River   Lippstadt
FIRST (PART)   Dortmund
Ruhr River   B
GERMAN   SEVENTH
REICH   Werra R.
FIFTEENTH
US FIRST   Fulda R.
US THIRD
Main R.
FIRST
G

Hanover

Legend
- ꟿꟿꟿ WEST WALL
- ••••• FRONT FEB. 8, 1945
- ××××× FRONT MARCH 5, 1945
- ▭▭ FRONT MARCH 10, 1945
- ----- FRONT MARCH 21, 1945
- ——— FRONT APRIL 4, 1945

0   25   50 mi
0   25   50 km

After the failure of Hitler's Ardennes counteroffensive, Field Marshal Gerd von Rundstedt, commander in chief West, re-formed his battered forces behind the West Wall. In February and March, the Allied forces breached the wall and advanced to the Rhine River. Rundstedt's defense of the Rhineland had cost the Germans another 60,000 men killed and wounded in addition to 250,000 prisoners—a blow from which the German army could not recover. On March 7, elements of the U.S. First Army seized a bridge over the Rhine at Remagen. Fighting with inadequate forces, the Germans were unable to halt the Allied breakouts from their Rhine bridgeheads, and soon the Allied armies were surging across western Germany. By the beginning of April, the German forces were in complete disorder. Army Group G fell back to the Danube, but Army Group B remained trapped in the Ruhr.

A German soldier lies dead on the rocky shore of the Rhine River as American troops splash ashore from their landing craft. By March 28, 1945, the Allied troops had secured six major bridgeheads across the Rhine.

which the Germans narrowed further by breaching the Rhine banks and flooding the adjacent low ground. The Allied plan called for a thrust into the Reichswald on the evening of February 8 by the Canadian First Army, followed two days later by a second strike farther south, in the Roer River area, by the U.S. Ninth Army.

"We now fight on German soil," Montgomery told his men on the eve of the battle. "We have got our opponent where we want him." After a bombing raid on the cities of Cleves and Goch just beyond the Reichswald, the attack began with the most intense artillery bombardment unleashed on the western front during the entire war, a cannonade of half a million shells that lasted five and a half hours. When it finally stopped, five divisions of infantry advanced into the woods on a seven-mile-wide front, and the leading division captured Cleves on the second day.

The Germans now played their only remaining card. Before the second prong of the offensive could attack on February 10, they destroyed the discharge valves on the Roer River dams, thus ensuring that the Roer Valley would be flooded for at least two weeks. With the U.S. Ninth Army thus balked, Rundstedt was free to move his reserves into line against the British and Canadians. Allied momentum was slowed further by the boggy terrain and monstrous traffic jams that clogged the lone road through the Reichswald after reinforcements were prematurely ordered forward.

Rundstedt's troops, forbidden from withdrawing to the Rhine by a stand-at-all-costs order from Hitler, fought with Montgomery's forces through the two weeks of rain and mud. The breakthrough came when the Americans crossed the Roer on February 23. A week later, the Americans were on the west bank of the Rhine near Düsseldorf and had linked up with the Canadians to the north, threatening to cut off the Germans west of the river.

Hitler's orders forbidding withdrawal across the Rhine robbed his generals of their last chance to prepare an orderly defense. General Alfred Schlemm, commanding the veteran First Paratroop Army, was told that he was personally responsible for keeping the bridges along the northern Rhine out of enemy hands. If and when the Germans retreated across the river, the bridges were to be blown; any commander who allowed a bridge to be captured intact was to be shot. "Since I had nine bridges in my sector," Schlemm wryly told an American interrogator after the war, "I could see that my hopes for a long life were rapidly dwindling."

Schlemm shortened his perimeter and held off the Canadians and the British until March 10, when he destroyed the last two Wesel bridges and withdrew. His stubborn, foot-by-foot battle had won the admiration of his foes. A British general ordered his staff to stand "in respectful silence" as prisoners from the First Paratroop Army passed on to the rear.

The Allies made their first rush on a Rhine bridge on March 2, when soldiers from the U.S. 83d Infantry Division scrambled onto a span at Oberkassel, near Düsseldorf, just as it blew up. Two days later, the Americans came close again when the Germans destroyed the Adolf Hitler Bridge at Krefeld at the last minute. The U.S. First Army reached Cologne on March 5 only to find the bridges there blown as well; one of the Cologne bridges had been demolished prematurely, resulting in the capture of a large contingent of Germans west of the river.

On the afternoon of March 7, patrols from the U.S. 9th Armored Division gained a bluff overlooking the town of Remagen, fifteen miles south of Bonn on the Rhine, and saw to their surprise that the Ludendorff railway bridge was still intact, with German troops streaming across it. At 3:15 p.m., a German prisoner told the Americans that the bridge was to be destroyed at four o'clock. A few minutes later, an explosion sent a cloud of smoke rising from the western end of the bridge. When the smoke cleared there was a thirty-foot-wide crater in the roadway, but the bridge still stood. Moments later, another blast caused the bridge to quiver and rise, only to settle back into place.

American infantrymen and engineers darted onto the span after the second explosion. Engineers found four packages of TNT lashed to beams below the deck and quickly cut the wires, then located the control switch on the east bank of the river and destroyed it. By 4:15 p.m., the Rhine had been breached. Eisenhower promptly diverted five divisions to hold the bridgehead, and by March 8, the Americans had 8,000 men across along with their armor and artillery. Nine days later, the Remagen Bridge crumbled into the Rhine as a result of the cumulative punishment it had taken. Five German officers were condemned to death for allowing it to be captured. For Rundstedt, the loss of the bridge at Remagen represented the end of the war. Field Marshal Albert Kesselring replaced him as commander in chief West. "I am Germany's new secret weapon," Kesselring jokingly remarked to his staff.

On the southern sector of the front, in the area known as the Palatinate, the U.S. Third Army under Lieut. General George S. Patton crossed the Moselle River on March 14, uncovering the northern flank of the German First Army, and drove on toward the Rhine near Mainz. Patton's forward elements reached the Rhine at Oppenheim, fifteen miles south of Mainz, on the 20th and 21st. On the night of the 22d, six battalions crossed the river in assault boats with minimal casualties, and the engineers immediately erected a temporary bridge. By the following day, this second Rhine bridgehead was six miles deep and seven wide.

Hitler was more distressed by Patton's breakthrough at Oppenheim than

Field Marshal Walther Model congratulates three members of the Hitler Youth after awarding them the Iron Cross, Second Class, for bravery. Unable to prevent the Americans from overrunning his 317,000 troops trapped in the Ruhr pocket, Model committed suicide in a forest between Düsseldorf and Duisburg on April 21, 1945.

by the capture of the Remagen Bridge because the German force in the Oppenheim area was weaker. But when he requested that a panzer brigade be sent to Oppenheim, he was told that none was available, and for once Hitler could not argue: The western front had been stripped to the bone. In the battle for the Rhineland alone, 60,000 Germans had been killed or wounded and 293,000 captured.

One day after Patton's coup at Oppenheim, the western Allies mounted their largest and most carefully orchestrated offensive of the war's final weeks. Montgomery had amassed more than one million men and 3,300 guns west of the Rhine on either side of Wesel. Preliminary bombing raids on the Ruhr and the cities east of the Rhine had been going on for weeks. At seven o'clock in the evening on March 23, the big guns blasted a frightful overture. Two hours later, the crossings began. Winston Churchill, having arrived that afternoon in time for tea, watched the action beside Montgomery at the command post.

By dawn, the British prime minister was across the Rhine along with the troops, who had established three bridgeheads and advanced six miles against scattered resistance. With the main German force concentrated in the central Rhine Valley farther south, Montgomery could advance almost at will. A huge airborne drop added 14,000 paratroopers to his onrushing force. By March 28, Montgomery's northern bridgehead was thirty-five miles wide and just as deep. He had twenty divisions and 1,500 tanks on

the edge of the Westphalian plain, and the way to the Elbe and the Baltic lay open to him. The Canadian First Army turned north to cut off the Germans who remained in the Netherlands while the U.S. Ninth Army blocked the eastern and northern edges of the Ruhr, helping to bottle up the 250,000 troops in Model's Army Group B.

The circle around Model closed when the U.S. First Army met the Ninth Army on April 1 at Lippstadt. Even the great arms and oil installations in the Ruhr could not help Model now; they had been all but obliterated by Allied bombers. Army Group B, supported by another 100,000 men from a Luftwaffe antiaircraft command, fought on for two more weeks as their supplies of food and ammunition dwindled. On April 15, Major General Matthew B. Ridgway of the U.S. XVIII Airborne Corps sent a message to

American and Soviet soldiers shake hands in the middle of a broken bridge over the Elbe River at Torgau on April 25, 1945. By this date, the German high command had directed theater commanders to accept "greater losses of territory to the Anglo-Americans" in order to free troops to fight the Russians.

Model urging him to surrender "for the reputation of the German officer corps and for the sake of your nation's future." Model refused, citing his oath sworn to Hitler personally. That same day, the German commander ordered his troops to break out of the pocket in small groups.

By April 18, it was all over, and the Allies began sweeping in a haul of 317,000 prisoners—even more than the Russians had seized at Stalingrad. Model, however, was not among them. Accompanied by a half-dozen men, he managed to slip through Allied lines in the woods near Duisburg. On April 21, he walked into a thicket and shot himself. General Friedrich von Mellenthin, a staff officer assigned to a panzer army under Model, later claimed the field marshal had "tried several times to be killed in action."

The Ruhr, like so much of Europe, had been reduced to a virtual wasteland. "Not a house was unscarred by bombs," wrote Leonard Mosley, a British war correspondent who passed through the area a few weeks later. "Every factory was an ugly vista of torn and twisted steel. Great piles of bricks and boilers and derricks sprawled over yards and roads and railway lines." What surprised Mosley was the attitude of the civilians, who welcomed the Allies with cheers and "obvious happiness."

A forward unit of General Omar N. Bradley's Twelfth Army Group reached the Elbe at Magdeburg, fifty-three miles west of Berlin, on April 11. The Allies were now as close to Berlin as the Soviets were, and unlike the Soviets, they faced little opposition. Eisenhower, however, decided to shift his main thrust south toward what was believed—falsely, as it turned out—to be a last-ditch concentration of German strength in a mountainous area of Bavaria and Austria called the Alpine Redoubt. Churchill, eager to gain territorial leverage for the postwar conflicts he anticipated with Stalin, argued for a quick rush to Berlin, but the American high command insisted that the first priority was to destroy the remaining German armies: Berlin was left to the Russians.

In mid-April, the Allied advance ground to a halt in the center while Montgomery rolled on toward Hamburg and the Baltic, and Patton searched for the phantom legions of the Alpine Redoubt. On April 21, Eisenhower told the Soviets that he was stopping his armies on a line running from the Elbe and Mulde rivers to western Czechoslovakia. Bradley's divisions were sprawled along a 250-mile-wide front, creating a logistical nightmare. The Soviets, meanwhile, were grinding closer every day to the bunker beneath the chancellery.

On April 25, the same day the Russians closed the circle around Berlin, GIs from the U.S. First Army joined hands with Soviet soldiers from the Fifth Guards Army at Torgau on the Elbe River, seventy miles southwest of Berlin. The Third Reich was a fortnight away from its final reckoning. ✚

Chasing a Lost Cause in Hungary

While Adolf Hitler gambled away his forces in the Ardennes in late December 1944, the Red Army surged westward. On the day after Christmas, the Second and Third Ukrainian fronts encircled 188,000 German and Hungarian troops in Budapest. For weeks, Hitler had refused to send reinforcements to these beleaguered forces. Finally, in early January 1945, he shifted his armies on the western front to the defensive, freeing some of the best units for transfer to the east.

Intent on protecting the Hungarian oil fields southwest of Lake Balaton (*map, inset*), which provided up to 80 percent of the Reich's remaining fuel supplies, Hitler committed his last operational reserve, the Sixth SS Panzer Army, to a final offensive in Hungary. Led by long-time Nazi loyalist SS General Sepp Dietrich, the 100,000-man force had recently been withdrawn from the failed Ardennes offensive, where it had shouldered the burden of the main attack. Now, it was charged with the daunting task of pushing the Russians back across the Danube River.

General Heinz Guderian, the army chief of staff, argued vehemently for sending Dietrich's troops to Germany's eastern border where a Russian spearhead was advancing toward the Oder River. But Hitler was obsessed with saving the oil fields. Without this source of oil, he told Guderian, "your tanks won't be able to move, and the airplanes won't be able to fly."

Implementation of the offensive had to wait until early March owing to the difficulties in transporting Dietrich's forces halfway across Europe on the bomb-damaged railroads. Meanwhile, Hitler failed to consider the pointlessness of his plan: Even if the Germans succeeded in gaining the territory, they no longer had the strength to hold it. "The eastern front is like a house of cards," Guderian warned his Führer. "If the front is broken through at one point, all the rest will collapse."

Panzergrenadiers riding in a half-track in the area between Lake Balaton and the Danube River approach a burning Russian vehicle in January of 1945. They were among the 220,000 Germans confronting a Red Army force of 407,000 in Hungary.

A German reconnaissance team (*below*) pauses on a snowy Hungarian road in early 1945. A wrecked American-made Sherman tank (*inset*), surrounded by dead members of its Russian crew, sits in the road leading to a village near Szekesfehervar. The Allies quickly replaced lost Red Army equipment. "More and more often," noted a Waffen-SS officer, "we faced Sherman, Churchill, and Cromwell tanks, which had been thrown into action without even having their English markings removed."

Sparring in the Triangle

At dawn on New Year's Day, 1945, the Totenkopf and Wiking divisions of the IV SS Panzer Corps mounted a counterattack across the Vertes Mountains northwest of Budapest. General Guderian later wrote that "neither the troops nor their commanders possessed the same drive as in the old days." The once ferocious SS units sparred inconclusively with the Red Army throughout January and February in the 435-square-mile triangle of land formed by Budapest and the strategic cities of Esztergom to the northwest and Szekesfehervar to the south, near Lake Velence.

On February 13, Budapest fell to the Red Army. Four days later, the I SS Panzer Corps, which was composed of the reconstituted Hitlerjugend Division and the Leibstandarte Adolf Hitler, retaliated by smashing through the Russian defenses at the Hron River bridgehead near Esztergom. Meanwhile, German troops assembled north and south of Lake Balaton to await the arrival of Dietrich's Sixth SS Panzer Army for what proved to be the last German offensive of the war.

A Panther tank crew (*above*) prepares to cross the Parizy Canal near Esztergom in February of 1945. The tank was part of a German armored force that surprised the Red Army at the Hron River bridgehead.

An SS motorcyclist (*inset, top left*) savors a cigarette after breaking through the Soviet siege lines surrounding Budapest. Of the 16,000 German survivors who tried to fight their way out of the capital in February 1945, fewer than 800 made it to safety.

Near Lake Balaton, a member of the Totenkopf Division (*inset, top right*) examines a Russian rifle that was abandoned in a trench formerly occupied by the Soviets.

A motorized column of the Sixth SS Panzer Army is mired on a road near Simontornya, east of Lake Balaton. The Germans took Simontornya on March 12 but lacked the strength to hold it.

SS General Sepp Dietrich (*seated, inset*) confers with one of his field police. Standing behind Dietrich is his aide, Captain Hermann Weiser, who was killed in action a short time afterward.

The Last Offensive

On the morning of March 6, 1945, fifteen divisions from Lieut. General Hermann Balck's Sixth Army and General Sepp Dietrich's Sixth SS Panzer Army sliced southeastward between Lake Balaton and Lake Velence, signaling the beginning of the offensive that was optimistically dubbed Frühlingserwachen, or Spring Awakening.

The two German armies initially pierced the Russian line, but stiff resistance slowed their progress, and they bogged down in the spring mud, their morale flagging. General Fyodor Tolbukhin, commander of the Third Ukrainian Front, seized the moment to counterattack. On March 17, the Russians broke the German front. Dietrich and Balck retreated toward the Austrian border—against Hitler's longstanding orders to fight to the last man. In a rage, the Führer demanded that the offending SS divisions be stripped of their honorary cuff titles. By that action, "we were left to our own fate," wrote one of Dietrich's officers. "What remained was immeasurable disappointment and bitterness."

Retreat from Vienna

By the end of March, the German armies were losing their tenuous grip on the area around Lake Balaton. After tens of thousands of Hungarian troops deserted, the Red Army slipped through a gap in the Hungarian-held sector of the front and wheeled into Austria. Hitler still refused to give up—even after the Nagykanizsa oil fields fell to the Russians on April 2. Instead, he ordered Sepp Dietrich to defend Vienna. Dietrich's army was shattered, however. "We still call ourselves the Sixth Panzer Army," Dietrich wryly remarked, "because we have six tanks left!"

On April 13, the Second and Third Ukrainian fronts occupied the Austrian capital. The Germans retreated to Saint Pölten, thirty miles to the west, where they were able to hold out for another two weeks. "A mass escape to the west then began," reported one SS officer. "But only a few managed to get through. Most were stopped by American tank units and handed over to the Russians. A slow death from internment, hunger, and misery awaited them."

After receiving orders from SS General Otto Weidinger (*wearing the overcoat at left*), three members of the Der Führer Regiment prepare to take up positions near the Floridsdorfer Bridge—the last bridge in Vienna to be blown up by the retreating Germans.

The commander of the Leibstandarte Adolf Hitler, SS Lieut. Colonel Joachim Peiper (*inset, wearing the brimmed cap*), confers with one of his unit commanders the day after Vienna fell to the Russians.

Atrocities that Outraged the World

"I had tried to visualize the interior of the concentration camp, but I had not imagined it like this. Nor had I imagined the strange, simian throng who crowded to the barbed-wire fences surrounding the compounds, with their shaven heads and obscene striped penitentiary suits. So wrote Derek Sington, the first British officer to enter Bergen-Belsen, the notorious camp in northern Germany. When Sington rode through the camp gates on April 15, 1945, he found 60,000 inmates hovering on the edge of death and another 13,000 already dead, strewn amid the filth that carpeted the cramped grounds. "We had experienced gratitude and welcome in France, Belgium, and Holland," Sington wrote. "But the half-credulous cheers of these almost lost men who had once been Polish officers, land workers in the Ukraine, Budapest doctors, and students in France, impelled a stronger emotion, and I had to fight back my tears."

The macabre scene was repeated again and again that spring as the Allies overran camps at scores of other hitherto obscure German localities. All told, they freed 715,000 prisoners. In every camp, disease was rampant, starvation almost universal. "How tragic it was that the great majority did not even realize that we were free," recalled one survivor. "They were unconscious or too sick to understand what was happening."

Earlier in the war, when the Soviets liberated the extermination camps in the east, they found only a handful of prisoners still alive. The SS had marched most of the largely Jewish camp populations to the west; those who survived the march were dumped into the concentration camps, which previously had maintained marginal sanitation. The overcrowding brought health conditions to an all-time low in the months before liberation.

Under orders from the Allied military command, the liberating troops forced German civilians to witness the results of the Nazi regime's heinous crimes. A number of SS guards were sooner or later brought to justice. But these measures were little consolation to the shattered inmates. "For the greatest part of the liberated Jews, there was no ecstasy," wrote one victim. "We had lost our families, our homes. We had no place to go, nobody to hug. We had been liberated from death and the fear of death, but not from the fear of life."

Prisoners in varying states of health stumble out of their barracks at Wöbbelin, a makeshift transit camp in northern Germany for evacuees from the east. The camp was liberated by the British Second Army and the U.S. 82d Airborne Division.

Confronting the Unimaginable

"Although you claim no knowledge of these atrocities, you are still individually and collectively responsible, for they were committed by a government elected to office by yourselves in 1933 and continued in office by your indifference to organized brutality," preached Reverend George Wood, a chaplain in the U.S. 82d Airborne Division, to the residents of Ludwigslust during his commemorative service homily for the Wöbbelin dead.

Wood was under orders from Allied military commanders who, in an attempt to refute the pervasive impression that "these things did not really happen," forced German citizens living in the vicinity of the camps to visit them and, in many cases, to help bury the dead. Civilians were rounded up and taken on tours of the camps, where they encountered pits filled with rotting corpses, ghastly instruments of torture, and crematory ovens.

The reaction of the Germans varied from shock, to grief, to indifference, to denial. One resident of the town of Dachau summed up the attitude of many when he commented: "It was all very horrible, but what could we do?"

American military police show German civilians a truckload of corpses at Buchenwald. A British colonel, guiding a similar tour at Bergen-Belsen, remarked: "Whatever you may suffer, it will not be one-hundredth part of what these poor people endured."

Townspeople of Ludwigslust serve as pallbearers for the Wöbbelin dead. Many of the civilians wept, and one of them was heard to say: "It is a disgrace to be a German."

A dead SS officer drifts in a shallow river at Dachau where the inmates threw his body after they killed him.

When "Supermen" Became Cowards

By the time Allied troops reached the camps, most of the SS officials and their families had fled, leaving behind just a few dozen guards.

Years of suppressed rage drove some inmates, even in their weakened state, to exact swift vengeance. They killed a number of guards with their bare hands and beat others. A few SS men donned prison garb and tried to slip into the crowd, but their relatively robust appearance gave them away. For Simon Wiesenthal, a Mauthausen prisoner who later became a celebrated hunter of Nazi war crimi-

nals, it was an odd sight to see his former oppressors cowering in fear. "The supermen became cowards," he wrote, "the moment they were no longer protected by their guns."

American photographer Lee Miller said of the bloodied guards she saw at Buchenwald and Dachau: "Their condition is terrible, but they are still alive; and they are not so badly off as their new captors had been when beaten."

Some guards were fortunate enough to be taken into custody by Allied military police and kept in prison cells where, according to Miller, they "throw themselves on the floor for mercy every time the door opens." Several of them committed suicide. Most of the others were eventually brought to justice at war crimes trials.

Under British guard, SS women dump the skeletal remains of their victims into a huge burial pit at Bergen-Belsen.

113

Corpses spill out of a freight car on the tracks leading into Dachau. Allied liberators found a few barely conscious survivors among the moldering bodies.

Moral Evidence of Total Evil

Until Allied troops liberated the concentration camps inside Germany, many people in the west had been skeptical about the Soviet accounts of German atrocities in the east. After the Red Army liberated Majdanek near Lublin in eastern Poland in July 1944, for example, the New York *Herald Tribune* ended its story with the caveat: "Maybe we should wait for further corroboration. Even on top of all we have been taught of the maniacal Nazi ruthlessness, this tale sounds inconceivable." Now, there could no longer be a shred of doubt.

When Allied soldiers discovered the yellowed corpses stacked like cordwood, touched the skeletal hands of hollow-eyed children, and breathed in the stench of rotting flesh, all question of the total evil of nazism vanished.

For the former inmates, the horror continued well beyond the initial relief of freedom. When the British liberated Bergen-Belsen, the inmates were dying at a rate of 500 per day. Although many were saved by the greatest mass administration of blood transfusions, glucose, and antityphus injections in history, thousands more perished during their first few weeks of freedom. And those who remained were haunted by flashbacks of the unspeakable terrors of camp life, cursed with what one of them called a "submerged sense of guilt for having survived."

Bones and charred human remains fill the crematory ovens at Buchenwald. The Germans kept the oven fires burning right up until the arrival of the Allies.

THREE

End of the Twisted Dream

The afternoon of April 20, 1945, five days before the Soviet encirclement of Berlin, Adolf Hitler emerged from his underground bunker for the final time. It was his fifty-sixth birthday, and for the occasion, he climbed the stairs to the Reich Chancellery with its ruined and dusty rooms. Earlier in the day, the Allies had delivered their own lethal felicitations. The Americans and the British, with 1,000 planes, staged what would be their last bombing raid against the German capital, while approaching Soviet artillery units launched their first shells into downtown Berlin. "Unhappily," the Führer's secretary, Martin Bormann, noted in his diary, "the situation is anything but festive."

Hitler's birthday had been observed as a national holiday ever since his accession to power in 1933, but now Germany scarcely existed as a national entity. Only a narrow strip of German-occupied land linked north and south, and soon that would be severed by the junction of the Soviet and American spearheads. Berlin, bracing for the Soviet onslaught, was a bombed-out ruin, with its electricity, gas, and sanitation systems destroyed and the citizenry standing in line just to get food.

Hitler, too, was a wreck of his former self. His once-lustrous blue eyes were bloodshot and glazed, his brown hair turned ashen gray, his vigorous walk now a pitiful shuffle. "He seemed to be aging at least five full years for every calendar year," recalled Captain Peter Hartmann, a young member of his SS bodyguard. "He seemed closer to seventy than to fifty-six."

Nonetheless, the subdued birthday celebration provided the setting for a final gathering of the German and Nazi leadership. The bull-necked Bormann; the propaganda minister, Joseph Goebbels; the Reichsführer-SS, Heinrich Himmler; the foreign minister, Joachim von Ribbentrop; the armaments minister, Albert Speer; the military chiefs, including Grand Admiral Karl Dönitz, Field Marshal Wilhelm Keitel, and Reich Marshal Hermann Göring—all were assembled to shake hands and show loyalty to the chief. Göring, as usual, stood out. But instead of sporting his typical resplendent white linen or silver-gray outfit, he wore a simple uniform of olive drab that, someone whispered suspiciously to Speer, made Göring look

Surrounded by aides, a stooped and haggard Adolf Hitler arrives at the Reich Chancellery in Berlin in the late winter of 1945. The final months of the war exacted a heavy toll on the Nazi dictator. "All his movements were those of a sick, almost senile old man," one officer remarked. "His face spoke of total weariness and exhaustion."

"like an American general." Hitler received them all cordially but awkwardly in these reduced circumstances. No champagne was served. "No one knew quite what to say," Speer wrote later.

Presently, with his left arm hanging slackly at his side and his body listing to the left, Hitler limped outside into the wreckage-littered chancellery garden. A score of teenage boys were waiting there in uniform, drawn up in ranks at rigid attention. These tender warriors, members of the Hitler Youth, had come from Breslau and Dresden to defend Berlin with hand-held Panzerfaust antitank guns and to man the air defense batteries. While the newsreel cameras ground away, Hitler decorated the boys for courage shown on the Oder front, muttered a few words in a low voice, and with his trembling right hand, patted their beardless cheeks.

Afterward, he led the way back down into the bunker for the regular afternoon situation conference. His old cronies crowded around the big map while their Führer talked of the nonexistent German armies that would crack the ring of steel being clamped around Berlin by the Red Army. Then, the majority of his disciples departed. Himmler, Ribbentrop, Speer, and Dönitz went north. Göring, who already had arranged for the demolition of his nearby estate, Karinhall, after having evacuated its art treasures by the trainload, went south to his villa near Hitler's Bavarian mountain retreat at Berchtesgaden.

These were the forces on which the fragile fate of the Third Reich now rested: some young boys, a few armies phantom and real, the fanatical Führer in his bunker, and this old Nazi elite, now "splitting asunder"—in Speer's words—and heading off to plot last-minute maneuvers to save Germany or themselves.

Hitler's own fanaticism was fundamental to Germany's continued resistance. The Reich had been doomed at least since the previous summer when the Allies blasted out of their beachheads in France and the resurgent Red Army broke out of its own borders and drove westward. But those Germans who had seen defeat coming and had tried to stop the war by assassinating Hitler in his field headquarters on July 20, 1944, had only prolonged the suffering.

Hitler's escape from death in the bomb plot actually revived the popularity of his Nazi regime. The people had long ago made their Faustian pact with the Führer, and although their adoration had faded, his seemingly miraculous survival rekindled their hope that he could somehow save the Reich. Moreover, his survival reinforced his own relentless will. It was a "confirmation of the task imposed upon me by Providence," he told the people in a nationwide broadcast the day after the assassination attempt.

On his fifty-sixth and final birthday, April 20, 1945, the Führer congratulates members of the Hitler Youth, who have assembled in the Reich Chancellery garden to be decorated for bravery. The brief ceremony was Hitler's last public appearance.

Thereafter, he was more certain than ever of his own omnipotent powers. Any setbacks in the war were the result of sabotage and betrayal by the generals and their ilk who had initiated the conspiracy against him. "I am more than ever convinced," he confided to Mussolini, "that I am destined to carry on our great common cause to a happy conclusion."

To carry on this hopeless cause, Hitler increasingly relied on a narrowing circle of advisers. His deputy Göring had long since been discredited by the abject failure of the Luftwaffe to defend German cities against Allied bombers. "At the situation conferences," Speer wrote, "Hitler habitually denounced him in the most violent and insulting language." And with the exception of sycophants such as Field Marshal Wilhelm Keitel, Hitler now regarded his generals with unconcealed distrust and scorn. For the unquestioning obedience necessary to galvanize the last-ditch defense of the Reich, he looked to the triumvirate of Himmler, Goebbels, and Bormann.

Himmler was the evident principal beneficiary of the failed putsch. Already the wielder of extraordinary powers, Himmler was minister of interior, chief of police, and boss of the regime's racial policies in addition to his post as head of the SS. His SS empire, which most recently had absorbed the Abwehr, the armed forces foreign intelligence office, embraced a multitude of functions, from fighting under the banner of the Waffen-SS to operating thirty-six major concentration and extermination camps, as well as scores of holding pens and transit camps, and killing millions of Jews, Slavs, and other prisoners.

Within hours of the attempted assassination, Hitler assigned Himmler the tasks of crushing the conspiracy responsible for it and then restructuring the army. For the latter assignment, he named Himmler commander in chief of the Reserve Army, giving him control of all military forces within the Reich and the responsibility for training all troops and formations prior to deployment on the battlefronts. The humiliation of the regular army was so complete that no general breathed even a word of protest at the ascension of the man the old officer corps hated above all others.

Ever the energetic bureaucrat, Himmler began the training of 500,000 fresh recruits culled from German industry. His predecessor had been scraping together new units by scouring hospitals and convalescent homes for men previously thought unfit for duty. The need for manpower became particularly acute, however, after the first American patrol penetrated the German border on September 11, and the cry went forth to wage a *Volkskrieg*, or People's War.

Himmler's special contribution was to raise some twenty new volks-grenadier divisions. These people's infantry units were patched together from fragments of existing divisions as well as new conscripts, men from supply depots, and assorted desk soldiers. They were staffed with young officers who had little experience but displayed a fervent Nazi spirit. The Nazi daily newspaper *Völkischer Beobachter* praised the units as a "true marriage between party and Wehrmacht." But they proved to be poorly trained, and many of them were of little use in the field.

As chief of the Reserve Army, Himmler also was responsible for training and equipping the new People's Army, or Volkssturm. This militia, created in October to defend the homeland, drafted more than one million men and boys aged sixteen to sixty who otherwise had been exempt from conscription. To the dismay of military men, the Nazi party exercised direct control over the recruiting of the Volkssturm, which trained one day a week with dummy weapons and a large dose of ideology. Heinz Guderian later wrote in disgust of a retired general who was required to serve in the rank and file of a Volkssturm company that was "commanded by some worthless party functionary." Guderian noted that in the Volkssturm drill, the "proper way of giving the Hitler salute" often took priority over training in basic weapons and tactics.

Himmler brought to his new military responsibilities the old arsenal of terror and intimidation that had been perfected by the SS as well as its security apparatus. He established summary courts-martial to try and then execute soldiers who deserted their units—and he threatened to shoot even the families of deserters. His spies and informers also helped root out officers accused of infractions less clearly defined—so-called saboteurs of the war effort. A colonel was reported "lax in his attitude to duty and should

Heinrich Himmler *(left)* **discusses with army officers and civilian dignitaries the workings of a "trackwolf," a device used to rip up railroad ties. After the July assassination plot, Hitler so distrusted his officer corps that he gave Himmler command of the Reserve Army—although the SS chief's total military experience consisted of a few months' duty as a cadet during World War I.**

be dismissed"; another officer was "politically colorless"; yet another was "said to have a Jewish grandmother."

At every turn, Himmler acquired titles and power. He took over from the armed forces authority for all prisoner-of-war camps. He usurped from the Luftwaffe control of the development and production of the V-2 rockets. In August, his SS minions had cruelly put down the uprising of the Warsaw underground; in October, his operatives staged a coup in Budapest to keep the Hungarian allies in line. He eventually was given command of two different army groups. His position as the heir apparent seemed all but confirmed in November when Hitler selected him to deliver the speech commemorating the Beer Hall Putsch of 1923.

Goebbels also emerged from the abortive assassination plot with enhanced powers. For more than a year, he had been criticizing German laxity and urging Hitler to endow someone—preferably Goebbels himself—with sweeping powers to galvanize the home front for all-out war. On July 22, 1944, three days after he escaped the exploding bomb at Wolfsschanze, the Führer named Goebbels to the new post of General Plenipotentiary for Mobilization of Total War. The timing caused Goebbels to quip to an assistant: "It takes a bomb under his arse to make Hitler see reason."

Goebbels's mandate was to tighten up the German economy so efficiently that he could shake out one million new soldiers for the Wehrmacht in a period of three months. He soon issued a barrage of wide-ranging decrees aimed at waging what he called total war. These new laws introduced the sixty-hour workweek, restricted nonessential travel, reduced mail deliveries to one a day, shut down almost all theaters and luxury shops, halted publication of most periodicals, and suspended school for adolescents fourteen and older in order to free them to operate antiaircraft guns.

He directed the most radical decrees at women. Throughout the war, Hitler had been determined to keep women in the home. As a result, the number of females employed outside the home had increased by only 182,000 in five years; the number working in industry had actually decreased. In fact, German households employed just as many domestic servants as before the war. Under the slogan "The German Woman Helps Win," Goebbels sought to change all this. His new decrees practically eliminated housemaids and obligated all women under the age of fifty to perform work outside the home.

Mobilization of German women met with mixed success, even in Goebbels's own household. During the autumn of 1944, he had 250,000 girls and women operating searchlights and serving in other ways as noncombatant auxiliaries to the Wehrmacht. Goebbels's own wife Magda volunteered for a time at the Telefunken Radio factory, traveling there by trolley rather than limousine before tiring of it when wives of other party leaders failed to follow her praiseworthy example. Similarly, little came of Goebbels's scheme to set up a home workshop to make shell fuses under Magda's supervision. But Goebbels managed to draft her for another task. After his beauticians were conscripted for the war effort, he assigned his wife the job of manicuring his fingernails every Friday.

In addition, Magda had to give up her household help. Goebbels released the cook and two maids to free them for factory work. Two days later, the cook returned to report that she had found employment in her specialty

A female firefighter practices her newly acquired skills. She was among the hundreds of thousands of German women who joined the work force in 1944 as part of a program organized by Goebbels to free more men for military service.

in the household of the Reich Commissioner for occupied Denmark in Copenhagen, Werner Best. "Goebbels heard of this and was furious," his assistant at the Propaganda Ministry, Rudolf Semmler, wrote in his diary. "He accused Best of sabotaging the total war effort. So now she has a job in the canteen at the Siemens works serving out beer."

Before the end of 1944, Goebbels had dredged up an additional 500,000 men for the army—half the number that he had promised Hitler. He also had patched together a potential new labor force of at least that many women. Ironically, many of these new workers sat idle. In fact, there was no real lack of workers. The Reich already had pressed into service some 7.5 million Soviet and other slave laborers and prisoners of war. And when German production of weapons began a precipitous decline after reaching a peak late in the summer of 1944, the problem was not manpower but shortages in raw materials and disruptions of the transportation system caused by Allied bombers.

To monitor popular reaction to his total war campaign—and to boost it where necessary—Goebbels borrowed a technique from his early days as a party organizer in Berlin during the late 1920s. His special *Aktion B* teams, each consisting of a speaker and two *Volksgenossen*, fellow party members, would visit restaurants and other public places to provoke a discussion. Any word of criticism of the war effort would be greeted with a physical beating from the indignant Volksgenossen.

In his other major role as Hitler's master propagandist, Goebbels stoked the embers of total war with words as well as decrees. He now laced the big lie with frank desperation. "We have to become a people of fanatics," he wrote on November 5, 1944, in the periodical *Das Reich*. The fanaticism that he envisioned would "course like a glowing lava through the entire people and ignite national passions to a raging fire of the most sacred and determined preparedness."

To stir the masses, Goebbels resorted increasingly to a pair of stock themes. One was the arsenal of secret weapons that would somehow snatch victory from defeat. These weapons ranged from the V-2 missiles unleashed against London in September to the Messerschmitt 262 jet fighter planes that made their debut early in 1945. These were important technological innovations, but once deployed, their secrecy evaporated, and their inability to make a dramatic difference became distressingly evident. Only a potentially decisive weapon like the atomic bomb possessed the power to turn the tide, and German scientists lagged some five years behind the Americans in nuclear research. All the same, Goebbels spoke fervently of having seen a hidden German arsenal that "made my heart stand still for a moment." He even created a special department within the Propaganda Ministry to spread rumors about death rays and other nonexistent weapons.

The other stock theme employed by Goebbels played on the growing fears of an enemy victory. Ever since the Allies formally set forth their demand for unconditional surrender at the Casablanca Conference in January 1943, Goebbels had harped on the consequences of a German failure. Defeat, he warned, meant that "we Germans will be condemned to be the slaves and mules of the whole world."

Alarm about Soviet intentions was extensive in Germany. Most Germans fully anticipated a terrible revenge from a people whom the Nazi regime had condemned as subhuman and treated as such. Then, as the Red Army rampaged through the Baltic States and entered East Prussia in the autumn of 1944, came the reports of widespread rape and other atrocities—not all of them exaggerated. These incidents, which Goebbels dubbed the "wildest excesses of a bestial soldiery," gave substance to his apocalyptic visions of a Europe whose "blooming cities will be turned into settlements of mud huts, its broad streets into country lanes."

At the same time, the Americans provided Goebbels with a grand opportunity to exploit the German fear of the western Allies as well. In late September 1944, the American press published details of a proposal developed by Secretary of the Treasury Henry Morgenthau, Jr., to strip postwar Germany of its industrial capacity and convert it into a "country primarily agricultural and pastoral in its character." The fact that Morgenthau happened to be Jewish endowed his idea with extra potency among a people whose leaders had sought to destroy the Jews. Goebbels could now credibly assert that the United States and Britain would prove no more lenient than the dreaded Soviets. Massive and apparently indiscriminate bombing raids on German cities by the British during that autumn only seemed to confirm his contention that the Allies wanted to turn the Reich into a "potato patch."

Goebbels began other propaganda campaigns based on little or no factual foundation. He created, for example, the myth of the Alpine Redoubt. Goebbels trumpeted that the Reich would make its last stand in Bavaria and Austria in mountain fortresses and underground factories and laboratories where German scientists were already working to produce the ultimate secret weapon. Although nothing resembling such a redoubt existed, reports of it helped influence the Americans to strike southward instead of continuing their drive eastward toward Berlin in the spring of 1945.

Nowhere in the dying days of the Reich did Goebbels's brazen artistry shine more brilliantly than in the creation of Operation Werewolf. Variously credited to Himmler, Bormann, and even Robert Ley, the German Labor

Front chief, Werewolf was a scheme in which the SS would prepare armed gangs of guerrillas—"werewolves"—to operate behind enemy lines. Beyond an abortive training program and isolated acts of individuals, Werewolf never materialized, except in Goebbels's vivid imagination. Hoping to inspire Germans to actually undertake such resistance and sow panic among the enemy, he created a special radio station to broadcast stories of sabotage and assassination carried out by nonexistent Werewolves.

Radio Werewolf actually was situated a few miles outside Berlin but melodramatically reported itself as located somewhere in occupied territory. Each day, Goebbels himself would dictate a dozen or so stories extolling the Werewolves' fictional activities and then stroll through the offices of the ministry, sardonically calling out: "Anyone got another Werewolf item?" It was a triumph of what he called "poetic truth," which he defined to an assistant as the description of events of the imagination that "should have taken place."

Goebbels's energetic efforts to mobilize the Reich regained for him the full approbation of the Führer. A notorious womanizer, he had lost favor just before the war when both he and Magda engaged in indiscreet extramarital liaisons. On January 30, 1945, Hitler rewarded Goebbels by naming him Defender of Berlin—the first public indication the Führer intended to defend the capital. It was Goebbels's city: He had helped win it originally as a party organizer and then ruled it as gauleiter. That same month, Hitler came to the Goebbels's house for tea, the first time he had visited his old prewar haunt in five years. It was an unmistakable sign that he had forgiven both Goebbels and Magda their indiscretions. The cautious Führer brought his own cakes and a thermos of tea. After his departure, Magda Goebbels proudly observed: "He wouldn't have gone to the Görings."

While Himmler garnered titles and Goebbels regained lost influence with the Führer, it was Bormann who consolidated the most power during the Reich's final phase. As Hitler's private secretary, he seldom left the Führer's side and controlled virtually all access to him. As chief of the party chancellery, he tightened his stranglehold over the party machinery right down to the *Blockleiter*, or block warden, and won for his subordinates—and himself—vast new authority. Unlike the other men around Hitler, Bormann's name was scarcely known to the German public. He was the ruthless, cunning but quiet master of political intrigue—the "Brown Eminence," a colleague said of him, "sitting in the shadows."

With Hitler's approval, Bormann pushed the tentacles of the party into every realm. After the failed attempt on Hitler's life, he placed Nazi political officers in all major military headquarters. He was instrumental in the

enforced suicide of Field Marshal Erwin Rommel and other army officers suspected in the failed putsch. Through the party, Bormann—not Himmler—actually controlled the Volkssturm People's Army; he and his gauleiters were responsible for the induction of its members and providing its political leadership.

Bormann revitalized the ranks of the gauleiters. He got rid of many of the old-line incompetents and replaced them with younger men to whom he gave sweeping powers. The gauleiters, for example, were given authority over most military matters within their jurisdictions, including the prosecution of soldiers who failed to fight. And a month after the assassination attempt, the armaments chief Speer yielded to Bormann and handed over responsibility for armaments production to the provincial leaders. Bormann also won the allegiance of Speer's closest associates. By January 1945, the party had so encroached upon Speer's authority that he was reduced to pleading with Bormann to prevent the gauleiters from confiscating and passing out desperately needed coal from the fuel trains that passed through their provinces.

The ascendancy of Bormann inspired dread and generated a series of shifting alliances within Hitler's inner circle. Göring was so afraid that Bormann would stage a putsch and have him assassinated that he kept a division of paratroopers on guard at Karinhall. Goebbels, after aligning himself with Himmler, eventually gravitated toward Bormann to form an odd couple: the party intellectual and the consummate bureaucrat.

The undermining of Himmler represented Bormann at his Machiavellian best. Aware of his rival's desire to prove himself as a soldier, Bormann arranged for his appointment as commander of the Upper Rhine Army Group on the western front and then of Army Group Vistula in the east. These field commands physically removed Himmler from the center of power and enabled Bormann to coopt several of the Reichsführer's top deputies, including Lieut. General Hermann Fegelein, the former jockey who had married Eva Braun's sister and served as Himmler's personal representative at Hitler's headquarters, and Ernst Kaltenbrunner, chief of the Reich security service. And, as Bormann had anticipated, Himmler's inexperience and the impossible military situation doomed his performance as a leader in the field. By March 1945, Himmler felt he had been reduced to such a failure in the eyes of the Führer that he took to his sickbed for a fortnight.

By then, Bormann clearly wielded the greatest influence over the Führer and appeared to be the quiet front runner in the succession race. As Germany's fortunes plummeted, Hitler became increasingly preoccupied with the question of his replacement. In mid-March, lunching alone with

In his customary position a few paces behind his master, Martin Bormann passes through camouflage netting to inspect a tiny model with Hitler. Bormann garnered political power and influence far beyond his modest title as secretary to the Führer: One bitter colleague called him the "Führer's Mephistopheles."

one of his female secretaries, he dismissed all the contenders, even Bormann. "I am lied to on all sides," he complained bitterly. "I can rely on no one. They all betray me. If anything happens to me, Germany will be left without a leader. I have no successor."

Hitler's own wretched physical and mental condition helped generate the widespread concern about a successor. He had emerged from the attempt on his life the previous summer with only minor injuries. But to Major General Walther Warlimont, General Alfred Jodl's deputy on the operations staff of the armed forces high command, "It seemed as if the shock had brought into the open all the evil of his nature, both physical and psychological." Hitler subsequently suffered so many different ailments—dental troubles, headaches, jaundice, stomach cramps, perhaps even a heart attack—that he spent three weeks in bed during September 1944. The tremors in his hands and left leg, which disappeared for a while after the bomb explosion, returned, leading several physicians, none of whom had examined Hitler, to conclude that he was afflicted with Parkinson's disease. His emotions, always mercurial, now swung wildly between rage and despondency.

The medication he took almost certainly contributed to Hitler's declining health. Hitler was a notorious hypochondriac, and his personal physician of nine years, Dr. Theodor Morell, obliged by administering at least twenty-eight different drugs to the Führer. Something of a quack who formerly served as a ship's doctor and as a venereal disease specialist among the bohemians of Berlin, Morell claimed that he had discovered penicillin only to have the secret stolen from him by British agents. He made a fortune from manufacturing chocolate vitamins and other nostrums, many of which he tried out first on the Führer. Among the medications he administered to Hitler were amphetamines, extracts from bull testicles, the poison strychnine, and probably morphine.

Whatever the causes of Hitler's mental and physical decline, he exacerbated his own problems by living underground. On January 16, 1945, after a massive Allied air raid, he moved permanently into the Führer Bunker, one of three subterranean shelters underlying the chancellery and its garden. It was a natural choice, for he feared not only the bombs but also assassins, as well as the infections he associated with fresh air and exercise. His new home was more than fifty feet belowground, protected by a concrete slab sixteen feet thick, and topped by six feet of earth. The bunker consisted of two levels and contained more than thirty tiny compartments that served as offices and living quarters. His entourage of generals, doctors, aides, secretaries, and bodyguards lived on the upper level or in the nearby bunkers under the government complex. Hitler spent most of his time on the lower level in his private, three-room suite and in the conference room next door with its large floor map.

He left the bunker only for an occasional conference in the chancellery and to walk his Alsatian Blondi at night. In seclusion behind the damp, musty concrete walls, he grew increasingly estranged from reality. He declined to see anyone who might bring bad news. When Goebbels sent him photographs documenting the Allied bombing of famous monuments and landmark buildings, he refused to look at them.

As Hitler's health declined, his nihilism grew stronger. He was determined to press on with the war no matter what the cost. His pronouncements echoed the words that he had spoken more than a decade before in 1934: "We shall not capitulate—no, never! We may be destroyed, but if we are, we shall drag a world with us—a world in flames." Goebbels, with his flair for the dramatic, fueled Hitler's destructive inclination with inflammatory rhetoric and volatile recommendations. He urged the Führer to use poisonous gases in the fighting, to repudiate the Geneva Convention governing the treatment of prisoners of war, and to execute thousands of British and American airmen in reprisal for the virtual leveling of Dresden

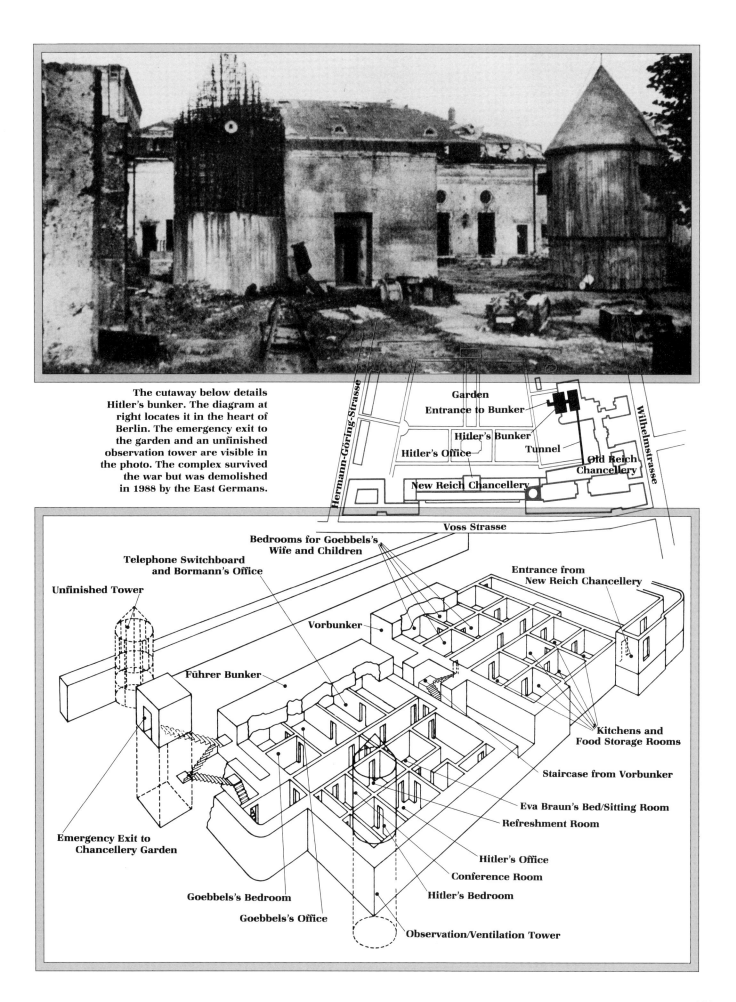

The cutaway below details Hitler's bunker. The diagram at right locates it in the heart of Berlin. The emergency exit to the garden and an unfinished observation tower are visible in the photo. The complex survived the war but was demolished in 1988 by the East Germans.

Hermann-Göring-Strasse

Garden
Entrance to Bunker
Hitler's Bunker
Hitler's Office
Tunnel
Old Reich Chancellery
New Reich Chancellery

Wilhelmstrasse

Voss Strasse

Bedrooms for Goebbels's Wife and Children

Telephone Switchboard and Bormann's Office

Unfinished Tower

Vorbunker

Entrance from New Reich Chancellery

Führer Bunker

Kitchens and Food Storage Rooms

Staircase from Vorbunker

Eva Braun's Bed/Sitting Room

Refreshment Room

Emergency Exit to Chancellery Garden

Hitler's Office

Conference Room

Goebbels's Bedroom

Hitler's Bedroom

Goebbels's Office

Observation/Ventilation Tower

by the Allies in February 1945. Hitler, surprisingly, carried out none of these measures but instead turned his cravings for destruction and catastrophe against his own people.

Perhaps the most potentially devastating of Hitler's nihilistic edicts was his so-called scorched earth policy. The practice of burning or otherwise destroying whatever might be of use to an advancing enemy was as old as war itself, and Hitler had issued such orders to his retreating armies in the Soviet Union as early as September 1943. But beginning in September 1944, as the enemy approached the German borders from both east and west, he had attempted to apply the policy to the Reich itself. Nothing but a desert would be left to the enemy, he decreed; not only farms and industrial plants would be torched and razed but also telephone networks, sewerage systems, and electric utilities—everything that was essential to the maintenance of an organized society.

It was this policy that finally seared the conscience of Albert Speer, the Führer's devoted architect and armaments minister. One of the few men around Hitler with noticeable moral sensitivity, Speer was also the archetypal technocrat; he had gone along with the war, happy to build factories and roads and design monolithic buildings. But now that the scorched earth policy threatened to bring down the world he had built, Speer began to act. Trying to avoid a head-on collision with the Führer, he quietly countermanded many of the orders for destruction, helping preserve mines and factories in Belgium and northern France as well as in Germany. By March 1945, Speer became so fearful that Hitler's course would disastrously undermine the postwar future of Germany that he hatched an assassination plot. But his plan to introduce poison gas into the ventilating system of the Führer's bunker was foiled by the unexpected construction of a protective chimney that put the air shaft opening out of reach.

Speer then decided to directly confront the Führer. Determined to "risk my head," as he later related, he wrote a blunt twenty-two-page memorandum to Hitler. "In four to eight weeks, the final collapse of the German economy must be expected with certainty," he declared flatly. "We must do everything to maintain, even if only in the most primitive manner, a basis for the existence of the nation to the last."

Three days later, on March 18, Speer went to the bunker to receive a photograph of the Führer in honor of Speer's fortieth birthday. Hitler penned a warm dedication on the picture, but then he delivered an icy retort to his architect's memorandum. "If the war is lost," he announced, "the people will be lost also. It is not necessary to worry about what the German people will need for elemental survival. On the contrary, it is best for us to destroy even these things. For this nation has proved itself to be

Displaying a spark of his old charisma on New Year's Day, 1945, Hitler regales *(from left)* armaments minister Albert Speer; OKW chief of operations General Alfred Jodl; OKW chief Field Marshal Wilhelm Keitel; and foreign minister Joachim von Ribbentrop. As Germany's fortunes waned, the Führer wanted the company only of advisers who agreed with him.

the weaker, and the future belongs solely to the stronger eastern nation. In any case, only those who are inferior will remain after the struggle, for the good have already been killed."

Hitler's even tougher written reply to Speer's plea was issued the following day in what came to be known as the Nero Decree. It ordered the destruction of "all military, transportation, communications, industrial, and supply facilities, as well as all resources within the Reich that the enemy might use either immediately or in the foreseeable future for continuing the war." Subsequent instructions from Bormann empowered the gauleiters to carry out the decree, took away most of Speer's remaining authority over industry, and although it would bring further chaos, ordered the evacuation of all cities and villages that lay in the path of the Allies.

Speer now pulled out every stop to thwart the decree. Racing around the Reich's rapidly shrinking domain with Hitler's personal chauffeur at the wheel—Hitler mistakenly had thought his driver's presence would deter Speer—the architect pleaded with plant managers, generals, and gauleiters. In the Ruhr Valley, he persuaded executives to bury in the watery sumps of coal mines the dynamite intended to demolish the mines; he promised submachine guns to arm local guards and factory officials to prevent demolition squads from destroying power plants and factories. In Heidelberg, he and his associates dutifully prepared copies of the gauleiter's orders to blow up every public utility in the state of Baden-Württemberg—and then deposited them in a mailbox in a town soon to be overrun by the Americans.

Through Bormann, Hitler learned of Speer's spirited odyssey and called him in. "If you were not my architect," he told Speer, "I would take the measures called for in such a case." The Führer tried to put him on sick leave; Speer refused. Hitler demanded he repudiate his contention that the war was lost. When Speer again refused, Hitler almost begged his old disciple: "If you could at least hope that we have not lost! That would be enough to satisfy me." Given twenty-four hours to think it over, Speer finally mollified the Führer by making a personal declaration of loyalty. Hitler was so touched that he even restored some of Speer's old authority and agreed to the "crippling" of industrial installations rather than their outright destruction. Thus armed, Speer went right on sabotaging what remained of the scorched earth policy.

In Hitler's eyes, Speer's defeatism was just as sinful as his actual deeds. The Führer still clung to his faith that the Reich would ultimately triumph. He predicted the enemy coalition would rupture, with the western powers turning against the Soviet Union and teaming up with Germany. Providence had saved him from the conspirators' bomb the previous summer; now he was counting on another miracle to provide surcease from the enemy armies besieging him.

Hitler frequently looked for solace in the historical example of his hero, Frederick the Great, whose portrait hung above his desk in the bunker. He would listen with tears in his eyes as Goebbels read aloud from Thomas Carlyle's biography of the eighteenth-century Prussian king who, like Hitler, had been confronted with catastrophe. In 1762, during the Seven Years' War, the Russians and five other foreign armies were on the verge of conquering Prussia. With all hope evidently vanquished, Frederick set a deadline for killing himself with poison. Then, three days before the deadline, his strongest opponent, Empress Elizabeth of Russia, died unexpectedly. The enemy alliance crumbled, and Frederick made peace with Elizabeth's nephew Peter III.

As a gloss on this inspiring tale, Goebbels dug up Hitler's old horoscope. Drawn up on the day Hitler first assumed power in 1933, the horoscope purportedly had accurately predicted the course of the war. It foretold the beginning of the war in 1939, the early German victories, and even the more recent devastating defeats. To Hitler's delight, the horoscope prophesied that Germany would score an overwhelming victory during the second half of April 1945 and then achieve peace in August.

On April 12, 1945, the American president Franklin D. Roosevelt died, and

The Ghastly Death of a Beautiful City

Dresden sparkles with all its gilded splendor in this pre-bombing photograph. The baroque Zwinger Palace is at left.

In early February 1945, thousands of refugees from the Reich's eastern provinces streamed into Dresden, swelling the city's population to more than 1.2 million. Having evaded the Red Army, they thought they had found a haven in the Saxony capital. Renowned for the fairy-tale beauty of its baroque architecture, Dresden had scant military significance. Although its industrial suburbs had been bombed a few times, the Germans were so certain that the city would not be targeted they had transferred its antiaircraft defenses to needier sites.

Thus, the surprise was total on the night of February 13 when 244 British bombers began dropping high-explosive and incendiary bombs on the city. Three hours later, an even more powerful armada struck, followed by waves of American planes. This triple onslaught from above unleashed firestorm winds with temperatures of more than 1,000 degrees Fahrenheit. The man-made hurricane sucked the oxygen out of the air and consumed everything in its path. The final death toll from the Dresden raid will never be known. The best German estimate is 135,000—nearly twice the number of people who died later that year in the atomic blast at Hiroshima.

Gutted buildings give mute testimony to the awesome power of the firestorm that engulfed eleven square miles of Dresden.

German soldiers and police try to identify bodies in Altmarkt Square before stacking them in pyres for burning.

A soldier prepares a mound of corpses for incineration. The ashes were later shoveled into carts and taken away for burial.

137

Goebbels was certain history was repeating itself. Here was the wondrous event that had been written in Carlyle's history and in the stars. He telephoned Hitler, who already was bustling around the bunker excitedly waving Roosevelt's newspaper obituary. "My Führer, I congratulate you," said Goebbels. "Fate has laid low your great enemy. God has not abandoned us. A miracle has happened."

Hitler at first planned to abandon Berlin to await the consequences of this miracle. He would go south to his alpine retreat at Berchtesgaden and continue the fight until the inevitable split between the Soviet Union and the West occurred. Although the fabled Alpine Redoubt was a Goebbels fabrication, workers had been laboring for a month to build extensive

Grand Admiral Karl Dönitz, Reich Marshal Hermann Göring, Field Marshal Wilhelm Keitel, and Reich Commissioner Artur Seyss-Inquart *(right to left)* **walk to a meeting in March 1945. After Göring fell into disfavor, Hitler made Dönitz his successor. The admiral served exactly twenty-three days—until the British arrested him on May 23, 1945, in Schleswig-Holstein where he had set up a government.**

fortifications there. Government ministries already had started moving to that area, and Hitler intended to go on his birthday, April 20. But despite the urging of Bormann and Göring, who pleaded with him to move while the slim corridor between the American and Russian forces remained open, the Führer hesitated. He wondered aloud how he could "call on the troops to undertake the decisive battle for Berlin if at the same moment I myself withdraw to safety."

Two days after his birthday, on Sunday, April 22, Hitler made up his mind. A counterattack he had ordered had failed to materialize, and the advance armor of the Russians had penetrated the city. Reports of these setbacks, delivered that afternoon at the military briefing threw him into a rage. Fists shaking furiously, tears streaming down his face, he cursed his assembled generals and railed again at treason and betrayal. "It is all over," he sobbed. "The war is lost. I shall shoot myself."

Hitler would stay in Berlin and meet his end there. Admiral Dönitz, one of the few officers he still trusted, would direct operations in the north from his base at Plön near the Baltic Sea. And if it came to negotiating with the Allies, Göring could accomplish that better than he could, Hitler decided. His generals tried to talk him out of it, reminding him of his duties toward the people and the Wehrmacht. But Hitler remained adamant, rendering his decision irrevocable by ordering a message to be broadcast to the people: "The Führer is in Berlin and will die fighting with his troops defending the capital city."

Hitler's sense of drama—and Goebbels's—had dictated the decision to stay. He and Goebbels had often talked about the concept of Götter-dämmerung (Twilight of the Gods). More than a Wagnerian opera of that name, Hitler's favorite, the story was deeply rooted in German mythology: All the gods, indeed all living things, would perish in a climactic battle with the powers of evil. Alone among Hitler's advisers, Goebbels wanted him to remain in Berlin for a spectacular finale that they would share. "When we leave this stage," he intoned dramatically, "then will the planet tremble."

At Hitler's invitation, on April 22, Goebbels moved into the bunker with his wife and six children. The five boys and one girl, ranging in age from four to thirteen, all had names beginning with the letter *H*, in honor of Hitler; to his delight, they called him Uncle Führer. Hitler's mistress, Eva Braun, already had been in residence underground for a week. Her presence and the arrival of the Goebbels sent a plain signal to the bunker staff. "Everyone could now read the handwriting on the wall," recalled Captain Helmut Beermann of Hitler's bodyguard. "The last act was about to begin."

Hitler's drama would be played out on his underground stage rather than on the streets he had vowed to defend. While the streets erupted with combat as the Red Army closed in, a strange calm settled over the Führer's catacomb. Bormann and several generals still made their way there each day from a nearby bunker, although the daily situation conferences that had consumed so much of Hitler's time and emotional energy no longer had any meaning. Hitler busied himself by selecting papers to burn. He was awake through most of the night, sleeping only three or four hours.

Much of the time, he lay on the narrow couch in his austerely furnished study. His once-spotless uniform jacket was now stained with food, and cake crumbs clung to his lips. He greedily gulped down chocolate cakes and played with the four puppies Blondi had whelped in March. His favorite was a male he personally trained and christened Wolf, his own old nickname. He would lie with Wolf on his lap, stroking the dog and repeating the name over and over again. He liked to quote Frederick the Great's remark: "Now that I know men, I prefer dogs."

Hitler could be instantly roused from his torpor, however. His moods jerked back and forth even more violently than before. The role of Dr. Morell's medications in these mood swings is uncertain. Morell left the bunker on April 22. "I don't need drugs to see me through," exclaimed Hitler. All the same, Morell left his nostrums with the Führer and may have given him a final round of injections before departing.

Hitler's temper exploded on April 23, the day after his decision to stay in the bunker to the end. Göring, now in his own villa at Berchtesgaden, had learned of Hitler's comment that the Reich marshal could do better at negotiations and had taken him at his word. Göring sent off a radio message to the Führer: "In view of your decision to remain at your post in the fortress of Berlin, do you agree that I take over, at once, the total leadership of the Reich, with full freedom of action at home and abroad, as your deputy, in accordance with your decree of 29 June 1941?"

Hitler was serenely reminiscing with Speer, who had come on a farewell visit, when the message arrived. Perhaps because it expressed Göring's personal loyalty, Hitler received the message calmly and resisted Bormann's efforts to depict it as treachery. But then Bormann got his hands on another communication from Göring, one informing the foreign minister, Joachim von Ribbentrop, of the possible succession. Bormann used this message to persuade Hitler that Göring's words amounted to a putsch against him. Thus incited, the Führer went into a rage and denounced his old disciple as lazy, a drug addict, and a "monumental crook." He agreed to Bormann's suggestions that Göring be stripped of all

This bookplate is from the library at the Berghof, Hitler's chalet at Berchtesgaden in southeastern Bavaria. Instead of seeking refuge there as most of his advisers urged, the Führer elected to remain in Berlin—a more heroic setting for his suicide than, as Albert Speer put it, a "weekend vacation retreat."

Hitler inspects bomb damage to the new Reich Chancellery on April 21, 1945. This was as close as he ever came to the reality of life in war-ravaged Berlin: From mid-January on, Hitler spent almost all of his time underground, insulated from the sufferings of the German people.

rank and office and arrested for high treason. But then Hitler slumped back into apathy. "Let Göring negotiate the surrender," he said. "If the war is lost anyhow, it doesn't matter who does it."

Nevertheless, Hitler stuck to the decision to sack Göring. And he proceeded to make the meaningless gesture of naming a successor as commander of the all but defunct Luftwaffe. Hitler selected one of the Reich's leading flyers, General Robert Ritter von Greim, a fifty-two-year-old veteran of World War I and pioneer fighter pilot. Greim had served as Hitler's personal pilot for a flight in 1920 during the short-lived Kapp Putsch. The journey ended in a forced landing short of their destination, leaving the future Führer with a dread of flying. But after Hitler took power, Greim was named the first squadron leader in the newly created Luftwaffe and later assumed numerous key commands.

Hitler was so oblivious to the chaos outside his bunker that instead of notifying Greim of his promotion by radio or telephone, he sent an urgent summons for his personal appearance. The summons arrived at Greim's base near Munich on April 24, but an Allied bombing raid delayed his departure. Accompanied by his mistress, Hanna Reitsch, a celebrated stunt flyer and test pilot, he reached the big air base at Rechlin, ninety miles north of Berlin, and was stranded there for a day. Finally, they commandeered a pilot and a Focke Wulf 190, a plane so small that the petite Reitsch had to crawl through an emergency opening into a cramped space in the rear of the fuselage. With an escort of some forty fighter planes, they headed toward Gatow, the only airport in the area still open, situated just west of Berlin. By the time they landed, the little plane's wings were riddled by Russian antiaircraft fire, and half of the fighter escort had been shot down.

For the last leg of the journey late on April 26, Greim took the controls of a Fieseler Storch reconnaissance plane. Reitsch sat behind him in the tiny two-seat cockpit while Greim flew just above the treetops to try to avoid Allied fighter attacks. Soviet infantry and armor had entered the city two days before and were fighting in the streets below. Suddenly, enemy flak punctured the fuel tank and smashed into the floor of the cockpit, severely wounding Greim in the right foot. When Greim fainted from loss of blood, Reitsch calmly leaned over his shoulder and grabbed the controls. Ten minutes later, she set the craft down in the heart of embattled Berlin, where trees and lampposts had been removed from the street to improvise a runway near the Brandenburg Gate. She hailed a car for herself and her wounded lover and rode to the bunker.

Such was the intrepid pair's adoration for Hitler that neither questioned the sacrifice of lives and planes required by his desire to personally promote Greim to field marshal and chief of an air force that now hardly existed. Reitsch regaled the Goebbels children with tales of flying and taught them to yodel. The wounded Greim was so entranced by Hitler's presence at his bedside in the bunker that he felt "as if I had drunk from the fountain of youth."

Greim's defrocked predecessor, Göring, was not the only Nazi leader who was in favor of immediate negotiations with the western Allies. Himmler, the disciple who always had proved so devoted that the Führer referred to him as *Treuer Heinrich* (Faithful Heinrich), was already deeply involved in the process. On the very night that Göring was sacked, Himmler, who considered himself Hitler's true heir apparent, held a meeting in the Baltic city of Lübeck with a Swedish intermediary in the hope of winning a separate peace from the West.

This parley with Count Folke Bernadotte of Wisborg, vice president of the Swedish Red Cross and nephew of the king of Sweden, culminated Himmler's gradual estrangement from Hitler. His alienation was influenced by two associates with differing motives. One was Felix Kersten, the Estonian-born Finnish masseur whose remarkable hands relieved Himmler's painful stomach cramps and whose humanitarian concerns chipped away at the Reichsführer's conscience. Thanks to Kersten and to Himmler's hope of impressing the West and preserving his own skin, many thousands of Jews and other prisoners were saved during the final months of the war. The other important influence was Walter Schellenberg, the shadowy former chief of counterintelligence and longtime Himmler deputy, who urged him to abandon Hitler, even murder him if necessary. Only by making a separate peace, perhaps using Europe's surviving Jews as hostages, Schellenberg argued, could Himmler and the SS survive to dominate postwar Germany.

The efforts of Kersten and Schellenberg brought Himmler and Bernadotte together at an SS hospital in northern Germany in February 1945. There, and at two subsequent secret meetings, the discussion centered on the release of Scandinavian Jews and others held in German concentration camps. Himmler was still so in thrall to Hitler that he could not bring himself to break with him or even to brook suggestions of disloyalty. He was shocked, for example, to learn on April 13 that his trusted former aide, General Karl Wolff, the SS leader in Italy, had been meeting with the American spy Allen Dulles in Switzerland—negotiating, it later turned out, for the capitulation of one million German soldiers in Italy.

Ultimately, however, Himmler felt liberated by Hitler's decision of April 22 to stay and die in Berlin. This, he said, released him from his loyalty to the Führer. On the following night, he and Bernadotte met in Berlin over candlelight in the Swedish consulate, where the electric power had been cut off. An air raid soon sent them to the consulate's bomb shelter, heightening the conspiratorial ambiance. Himmler related Hitler's intention to perish in Berlin. Anticipating his own succession, he authorized Bernadotte to inform the United States and Britain, through the Swedish government, of his willingness to surrender the Reich while continuing to fight the Russians until the western Allies had advanced to relieve German troops.

That done, Himmler spent the next few days working out in his mind all the details of his future proprietorship. He mulled over a name for the political party through which he would rule the postwar Reich and debated whether it would be proper to bow or shake hands when introduced to the supreme Allied commander, General Dwight D. Eisenhower. On Friday, April 27, four days after the candlelit rendezvous, his fantasy crumbled when he heard the devastating news from Bernadotte via Schellenberg: No such partial surrender was acceptable to the West.

Word of Himmler's peace feeler reached Hitler the following day via a news broadcast on Radio Stockholm, and it exploded in the bunker like a bombshell. To Hitler, Himmler's treachery was far worse than that of

After their dramatic flight from Munich to Berlin in late April 1945, Field Marshal Robert Ritter von Greim (*left*), the newly appointed chief of the Luftwaffe, and daredevil test pilot Hanna Reitsch wanted to die at Hitler's side, but Hitler would not allow it. One month later, Greim committed suicide, but Reitsch, the only woman to win the Iron Cross, lived on until 1979.

Göring, who at least had asked permission to take over. Faithful Heinrich, whose loyalty had always been above suspicion, had stabbed his Führer in the back. Hitler, his face livid with anger, raged that his disciple was guilty of treachery unparalleled in German history. He became so convinced of a widespread SS conspiracy against him that he ordered the execution of General Fegelein, Himmler's personal representative at Hitler's headquarters, who had slipped out of the bunker under suspicious circumstances two days previously. And to ensure that a "traitor never succeed me as Führer," he ordered the arrest of Himmler at his headquarters in the north.

Hitler entrusted this mission to Field Marshal Greim, his new Luftwaffe chief, and Hanna Reitsch. The two lovers wanted to stay and die with the Führer, who had greeted Reitsch two days before with vials of poison for herself and Greim in the event of an emergency. But Hitler insisted, and shortly after midnight that Saturday, Greim grabbed his crutches and hobbled up out of the bunker. Near the Brandenburg Gate, the same intrepid pilot who had flown them to Gatow two days previously was waiting in an Arado 96 trainer. It was a two-seater, so Reitsch squeezed in behind the seats. As they rose from the rubble-strewn street, the little plane flew into the glare of searchlights and barrages of small arms fire and flak from the embattled streets below. At 4,500 feet, however, they found cover in a cloud bank—a "fleecy, cumulus white," Reitsch wrote later in a rapture of romantic remembrance, "a giant quilt over the flaming and lost city."

En route north, Greim landed at Rechlin air base to try and carry out a second mission for the Führer. Hitler had ordered him to provide air support to help lift the Soviet siege of Berlin. Field Marshal Keitel and General Jodl had left the bunker nearly a week before to organize the relief effort. The Führer now believed that at least three different German relief columns were bearing down on the capital. In fact, many of the troops he counted on were already fleeing westward to surrender to the Americans. The only conceivable remaining hope was the newly organized Twelfth Army under Guderian's capable former adjutant, General Walther Wenck, which was fighting northeastward from the Elbe. For his part, Greim was able to muster precious few aircraft, and they made not an iota of difference against the overwhelming Allied superiority in the skies around Berlin.

In Berlin, these final days were more of a surrealistic nightmare than the star burst of Wagnerian glory envisioned by Hitler and Goebbels. Like their leaders in the bunker, much of the population—normally about four million but now swollen with the flood of refugees from the east—now lived underground. The people took refuge in shelters, cellars, and subway tunnels, venturing out only to seek food and water. In the rubble-clogged

Partially covered with tarpaulins, German fighter planes sit idle on an airfield. Although the Luftwaffe still had plenty of aircraft, there was almost no fuel to fly them.

streets above, corpses dangled from lampposts and trees, many decked with placards proclaiming their alleged cowardice or treachery. They were the victims of the so-called flying courts-martial conducted by SS men and party fanatics who chased them from the cellars and sentenced them to death for refusal to carry on the hopeless battle.

Those Germans who fought on were overwhelmingly outnumbered. Facing the one million or more Soviet troops that pressed in from all sides was a defense force that at its peak consisted of no more than 25,000 trained soldiers—fragments of two shattered divisions of the LVII Corps, two battalions of naval cadets airlifted in from the Baltic, a hodgepodge of SS formations including some French, Dutch, and Scandinavians, plus old men of the Volkssturm home guard and teenagers of the Hitler Youth. Practically all arms were in short supply except the Panzerfaust, which was still being manufactured in Berlin's factories and machine shops. These single-shot, antitank, grenade launchers were trundled through the streets in carts and passed out freely to untrained civilians who used them effectively to destroy hundreds of Soviet tanks.

The fighting intruded on Hitler's bunker when the Soviet gunners trained

their artillery on the chancellery. Slabs of masonry crashing into the garden above shook the bunker, and the intake pipes of the ventilating system sucked in so much dust and smoke that the system had to be shut down for up to an hour at a stretch. Exploding shells also periodically disrupted the bunker's radio and telephone links to the outside world. Reports from the city's defenders were frequently so confused and contradictory, Captain Gerhard Boldt recalled, that he and other army officers in the bunker had to resort to a last-gasp system for gathering intelligence about the enemy. They telephoned acquaintances or even people selected at random from likely addresses in the telephone book to ask: "Excuse me, madam, have you seen the Russians?"

By the early hours of Sunday, April 29, even as Greim soared aloft on his dual mission of arresting Himmler and scrambling the Luftwaffe to help relieve Berlin, the nightmare was closing in on the bunker. Hitler did not yet know it, but Wenck's Twelfth Army was bogged down twenty miles southwest of the capital. "Attack on Berlin is no longer possible," Wenck would signal later that day.

In Berlin, German-held ground had shrunk to a pocket less than nine miles long from east to west and not much more than one mile wide. Russian spearheads pierced the government quarter from north and south. Red Army units vied for the honor of storming the Reichstag, the charred

SS musicians serenade Eva Braun at the reception following her sister Gretl's wedding to an SS officer in June 1944. The Führer referred to his strawberry blond mistress and future bride as Tschapperl, an Austrian dialect word for "honeybun."

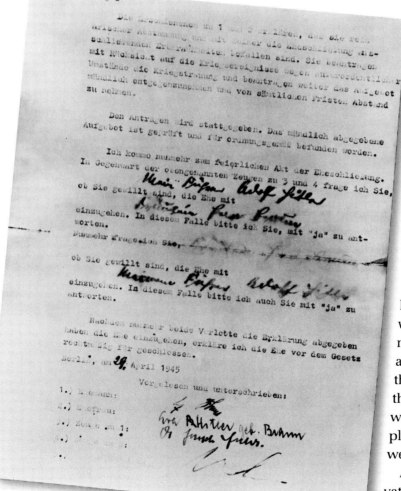

old parliament building that symbolized the Third Reich to the Russians, although it had not been used since 1933. Soviet tanks rumbled into Potsdamer Platz, scarcely a half-mile southwest of the chancellery, and less than a battalion of SS troops stood between them and Hitler's underground refuge. Reporting all this, General Helmuth Weidling, the last commandant of Berlin, presented a plan for Hitler to break out of the city. Hitler replied that such a temporary escape would only mean awaiting his end "somewhere under the open sky or in a farmhouse."

At that time, the Führer decided to take the final steps toward suicide. The deteriorating military crisis and above all Himmler's betrayal had triggered his decision. The first step, he wrote, would be to reward the "woman who after many years of true friendship came of her own free will to this city to share my fate." His old argument that marriage would interfere with his leadership of the Reich no longer had any meaning.

Early on the morning of the 29th, Hitler and Eva Braun met in the map room of the bunker. They stood before a middle-aged man in a Nazi uniform. He was Walter Wagner, a minor city and party official with the necessary notary authority who had been rustled up from his home guard post nearby. The groom wore his familiar field gray uniform; the bride wore a dress that Hitler favored—one made of black silk taffeta with gold clasps at the shoulder straps. Both swore that they were "of pure Aryan descent" and then, in the war-abbreviated version of the wedding ceremony, exchanged their simple vows. Bormann and Goebbels signed the wedding register as witnesses.

A reception followed in the Führer's private suite. The wedding party was joined by Frau Goebbels, secretaries, adjutants, and Hitler's vegetarian cook. The guests sipped champagne, ate liverwurst sandwiches, and talked about happier times. Walter Wagner, having stepped briefly from utter obscurity, took his leave and was shot dead as

he tried to return to his post on Wilhelmstrasse. At 2:00 a.m., Hitler and his secretary, Gertrud Junge, also left the reception, adjourning across the hall to a small study. There, Junge took shorthand while the Führer began dictating his last will and testament.

It was a disappointment. Junge later recalled that she had trembled with excitement at the prospect of hearing firsthand the Führer's own explanation for the war and the Reich's failure. But she and millions of others had heard it all before. He was not responsible for starting the war, Hitler asserted; it was the fault of the Jews. Nor was he responsible for losing it, he went on; that was the fault of the generals. Not one word of regret or remorse for his role in killing millions of people and bringing ruin upon the Reich passed his lips that night. Hitler seemed immune to guilt; eleven days earlier he had remarked: "If the German people lose this war, then they have shown themselves to be unworthy of me."

The only surprises in his testament related to the long-awaited succession. Göring and Himmler, of course, were banished from all offices of party and state "for their secret negotiations with the enemy" and "illegal attempts to seize power." Speer and Ribbentrop were also dropped from the cabinet. Goebbels was named chancellor and Bormann, "my most faithful party comrade," was appointed party minister and executor of his will. But Hitler's choice as chief of state, war minister, and supreme commander of the armed forces was none of these rivals who had so fiercely challenged one another over the years. Admiral Karl Dönitz, at fifty-four the longest-serving and ablest of the Wehrmacht commanders, was his choice to take the reins of the Reich. The selection made perfect sense even from Hitler's warped perspective. In his eyes, the army generals and the politicians and even the SS had betrayed him; hence, a sailor would succeed him.

Systematic preparations for suicide consumed the subsequent hours of that Sunday. Three couriers carrying copies of Hitler's last testament left the bunker charged with the mission of slipping through the Soviet lines and reaching Dönitz and two field commanders. (None reached his destination.) Hitler also ordered aides to make certain his body did not fall into enemy hands—a determination buttressed that day by word from Italy that his old ally, Mussolini, and the duce's mistress had been shot down by partisans and then strung up in the marketplace of Milan to be stoned and spat upon. That evening, he signed his last radio message, a plaintive plea for the whereabouts of General Wenck and the other relief columns. When there was no immediate reply, Bormann, smelling treason, radioed Dönitz, who had yet to learn the news of the succession: "The Führer orders you to proceed at once, instantly and unsparingly, against all traitors."

There was one further order. Hitler wanted to test the poison he in-

Joseph Goebbels and his wife Magda sit for a portrait with their six children and Harald Quandt (in *Luftwaffe uniform*), Magda's son from a previous marriage. On May 1, the day after Hitler's suicide, Goebbels and Magda killed their children and then themselves. Quandt, a prisoner of war in American hands, survived. The Soviets found Goebbels's charred remains (*bottom*) in the Reich Chancellery garden. The SS guards had lacked sufficient fuel to cremate his body.

tended to use. Shortly after midnight, the bunker's veterinarian and its dog trainer took Blondi into the Führer's bathroom. They placed an ampule of potassium cyanide in her mouth and broke it with forceps. Hitler came in afterward and regarded the corpse of his beloved dog with no visible show of emotion. Then the trainer, after bolstering himself with drink, shot Blondi's four pups, two other dogs, and his own dachshund. Hitler, before retiring, invited some twenty occupants of the two adjacent bunkers to join him in the conference room. He shook hands with each but said nothing.

Hitler slept for only an hour or so during his last night and arose before 6:00 a.m. on Monday, April 30. Before dressing, he summoned General Wilhelm Mohnke, the SS commander in charge of defending the bunker. Russian troops were only about 300 yards from the chancellery, Mohnke reported. His men could probably hold out another twenty-four hours; but then, May 1, the Communist holiday, the enemy would almost certainly mount a final mass attack. Hitler's personal pilot, General Hans Baur, also came by. He said a long-range transport was standing by at Rechlin to fly the Führer to Argentina or any other foreign refuge. Hitler ignored Baur's protests and presented him with his prized portrait of Frederick the Great.

After a routine military briefing later that morning, the Führer shared a simple lunch of spaghetti and tossed salad with his cook and two secretaries. His intimate associates were called together for one more leave-taking. He and Eva shook hands all around. "He whispered some words that I couldn't make out," Gertrud Junge said later. "I've never known what his last words to us were."

Shortly before 3:30 p.m., Hitler directed his spouse into their private apartment with a courtly gesture. They sat down on the blue-and-white velvet sofa in his study, only to be interrupted. Magda Goebbels hysterically lunged past the half-dozen people standing outside the closed door and burst into the room in a frantic attempt to dissuade Hitler from committing suicide. A couple of minutes later, she came out crying.

Hitler and Eva then proceeded with their carefully prearranged rites. They were well equipped. Hitler had two ampules of cyanide and two pistols; Eva had two similar capsules and a pistol. Each placed a capsule in the mouth. Hitler held the muzzle of his pistol to his right temple. He pulled the trigger and bit into the poison simultaneously. At the sound of the pistol, Eva too bit down. Thus, by their own choice, the Führer and his bride joined the tens of millions who had died in the war that he had brought down on the world.

SS men wrapped Hitler in a gray blanket and carried him up four flights of stairs to the chancellery garden. His wife, similarly enshrouded, was picked up by Bormann but snatched away by Hitler's chauffeur Erich

Red Army troops storm the Reichstag on April 30, 1945. The German parliament building, derided as the "lair of the fascist beast" by the Soviet propagandists, actually had stood gutted and empty since the 1933 fire that Hitler used to solidify his Nazi dictatorship.

Kempka, who knew that Eva had loathed the Führer's secretary. The corpses were placed in a shallow hollow in the garden and doused with nearly fifty gallons of gasoline siphoned from vehicles in the chancellery motor pool. From the shelter of a concrete canopy over the bunker exit, where the nine attending mourners took refuge from Soviet artillery, someone flung matches at the bodies, but the wind snuffed them out. Finally, Hitler's servant, Fritz Linge, twisted a piece of paper into a flare, lighted it, and handed it to Bormann. Bormann's first throw fell short, but the second landed on target, and a column of blue flame leaped above the bodies. As if on command, the mourners snapped to attention and flung their right arms skyward in a final salute.

They had failed to fulfill Hitler's order that the fire completely consume the bodies, however. So shortly before midnight, while the denizens of the bunker drank to the Führer and drew freely on their cigarettes—he had forbidden smoking—three soldiers were dispatched to the garden. Working to the recorded sounds of American Big Band music that blared from

the nearby enlisted men's canteen, they deepened a shell crater, dumped into it the charred remains of Adolf and Eva Hitler, and cov- ered over the crude grave.

Bormann and Goebbels delayed informing their new chief, Ad- miral Dönitz, of the Führer's death. They wanted to forestall further negotiations or machinations by Himmler, who was with Dönitz in the north at the town of Plön. They also wanted to negotiate their own temporary truce with the Red Army in Berlin, winning safe passage for Bormann to personally break the news to the new chief of state and gain influence with him. Their envoy, General Hans Krebs, the army acting chief of staff and former attaché in Moscow, made his way through the lines early on the morning of May 1 to present the nearest Soviet commander with the word of Hitler's death and the truce proposal.

When the Russians refused to budge from their demand for immediate unconditional surrender, Goebbels radioed the truth about Hitler and the succession to Dönitz that afternoon—twenty-four hours after the fact. At 9:30 p.m., Radio Hamburg, to the magisterial strains of Bruckner's Seventh Symphony and Wagner, reported the end of the Führer. Less than an hour later, Dönitz himself announced that Hitler had died fighting heroically "at the head of his troops."

It was a touch worthy of Goebbels, but that master deceiver already had followed his Führer to a fiery end. Disobeying Hitler's orders to leave Berlin and join the new government in the north, Goebbels had launched his long-planned final production about 5:00 p.m., some two hours after his message to Dönitz. It began, by one account, when a bunker physician administered lethal injections to the six Goebbels children; others said Magda herself put the children to sleep with doped chocolate and then poisoned them. A couple of hours later, Goebbels slipped on his hat, scarf, coat, and kid gloves and then climbed arm in arm with Magda to the garden. She bit into the cyanide. He shot her in the back of the head to make sure, then took his own capsule of poison and put a bullet into his right temple. Aides set the bodies afire with whatever gasoline they could find.

The remains, which would be found by Russian soldiers the following day, were still smoldering when Martin Bormann made his way out of the bunker that night. The consummate survivor, Bormann had no taste for the role of tragic hero. He joined SS men and others from the bunker in an attempt to sneak through subway tunnels and then break out of Berlin and

Field Marshal Wilhelm Keitel (*at right, below*) defiantly raises his swagger stick at the surrender to the Soviets on May 9, 1945, in Berlin. Germany had already capitulated to the western Allies.

join Dönitz. He and a companion, Ludwig Stumpfegger, one of the bunker physicians, managed to elude one detachment of Soviet soldiers who mistook them for stragglers from the Volkssturm home guard and offered them cigarettes. But later, during the early hours of May 2, another fugitive from the bunker came across Bormann and Stumpfegger lying on a bridge over railroad tracks a mile or so north of the bunker. They were sprawled there lifeless but with no obvious wounds. Evidently they had become trapped and had taken poison to avoid capture.

That same morning of May 2, Germany's new leader, Karl Dönitz—still astonished at the turn of events—shifted his headquarters to Flensburg near the Danish border to evade the rapid advance of the British. Though fervently loyal to the Führer, Dönitz, practically alone among Hitler's top subordinates, had harbored no political ambitions. He had assumed that Himmler would be Hitler's choice as successor; for that reason, and out of fear of the SS, he had refused to comply when Greim and Reitsch flew in three days earlier with Hitler's verbal orders to arrest the Reichsführer.

In any event, the glory of succession was long gone. Hitler had bequeathed Dönitz a legacy of ruin. The Greater Reich that had once dominated Europe all the way to the Urals now teetered on the brink of collapse. A shrunken and all but defeated Wehrmacht, about three million men, occupied Denmark and Norway, western Czechoslovakia, a handful of island outposts, and scattered, coastal strips or pockets in Yugoslavia, Holland, Austria, and Germany. Nearly half of Germany's fighting men were on the eastern front, retreating before the Soviet juggernaut.

With the bond of loyalty to the Führer now severed, Dönitz decided to end the war as quickly as possible. He was urged on by Albert Speer, who had originally suggested to Hitler that Dönitz be named his successor and who now turned up in the north as his closest adviser. But Dönitz wanted to delay a general surrender in order to, as he put it, "save the maximum number of Germans from Bolshevization and enslavement." This meant fighting on or prolonging negotiations for a week or more to allow time for troops and refugees to flee the eastern front and reach the jurisdiction of British and American forces. Independent piecemeal surrenders were already under way both east and west. The capitulation of German armies in Italy took effect at noon on May 2. That same day, the ranking official remaining in Berlin, General Weidling, formally gave up the city to the Soviets. And two days later, Dönitz's own representative agreed to the partial surrender to the British of German forces in northwest Europe.

But the pressure for complete capitulation mounted. Ironically, the fact that Hitler had bequeathed Dönitz both military and political control, naming him supreme commander as well as chief of state, conveniently set the stage for unconditional surrender. Still playing for time, Dönitz sent General Jodl to the supreme Allied headquarters at Rheims in France with instructions to stall as long as possible on complete capitulation. When General Eisenhower threatened to seal the British and American lines against Germans trying to surrender, Dönitz relented and agreed to the inevitable. At 2:41 a.m. on May 7, Jodl signed the instrument of unconditional surrender of all German forces on all fronts. Jodl, who would remain a Hitler loyalist to the end, stiffly praised the achievements and sufferings

Heinrich Himmler lies dead after biting into a cyanide capsule at a British army interrogation center near Hamburg on May 23, 1945. Failing to revive him with emetics and a stomach pump, the British wrapped Himmler's body in army blankets and camouflage netting, bound it with telephone wire, and then buried it in an unmarked grave.

of the German people and armed forces and expressed the hope "that the victor will treat them with generosity." To mollify the Soviet Union, a second signing was staged at Red Army headquarters near Berlin on the night of May 8. The surrender went into effect at midnight.

One by one, the men of Hitler's inner circle and the military commanders of the Reich were arrested by the Allies. Hermann Göring, still vainly seeking an audience with Eisenhower, was taken into custody near the Austrian border by American troops on May 7, the day of the Jodl surrender; he would later take poison to cheat the gallows after being convicted of war crimes during the Nuremberg trials. On May 23 at Flensburg, the British

rounded up Dönitz and Speer, both of whom would serve long prison terms, and Jodl, who would be executed.

And on that same day, the commandant of a British interrogation camp in northwestern Germany encountered a "small miserable-looking and shabbily dressed man." The prisoner had been arrested that morning at a British checkpoint near Bremen. He had a black patch over his left eye, wore a common German soldier's uniform, and carried the identity card of a field security policeman. As the British captain watched in astonishment, the man stepped forward, removed the eye patch, and put on the familiar rimless spectacles. In a quiet voice, he said simply, "Heinrich Himmler."

Here, so ignominiously displayed, was the high priest of terror, the man who had presided over the largest deliberate mass extermination in history. Perhaps more than anyone, even Hitler, he embodied the awful contradictions of Nazi Germany, the appearance of everyday banality that cloaked the most profound evil. He was after all, in Speer's memorable phrase, "half schoolmaster, half crank."

For the past three weeks, Himmler had been hovering anxiously about Flensburg, with his retinue of 150 staff members and personal fleet of big cars. He had been brought low from his high position as heir apparent. A failure in his negotiations with Count Bernadotte, disowned by his Führer, and disregarded by Dönitz whom he begged for a job in his new government, Himmler had put on the eye patch, shaved his mustache, and headed south on foot with a couple of aides and a few refugee field police, pretending to be Private Heinrich Hitzinger (the real Hitzinger had been condemned to death by the *Volksgericht*, or Nazi People's Court, set up in Berlin to render quick verdicts against traitors to the Reich).

Now, with his identity revealed, Himmler made certain he disclosed nothing more to British Intelligence. That night, while a physician searching him for poison turned Himmler's head for a better look, he clamped his jaw shut with a crunch. The vial of cyanide hidden between his molars broke, and the former Reichsführer-SS breathed his last. Himmler's finale, like that of his Führer, was no heroic, Wagnerian clash to the death, but a furtive escape by means of suicide.

Thus, after twelve years and a few months—far short of the 1,000 years prophesied by its late Führer—the Third Reich expired. Still to come were the trials at Nuremberg and the dispensation of justice to the surviving high Nazis for their crimes, but the long nightmare of genocide and war had reached its tragic conclusion. The scars would remain. The legacy of the Third Reich would haunt generations. What Hitler and his disciples wrought in little more than a decade would forever stand as a monument to man's capacity for inhumanity. ✚

The Indomitable Berliners' Ordeal

A Berlin street becomes a makeshift morgue after an Allied bombing attack in February 1945 killed 2,500 people and left 120,000 homeless.

On April 16, 1945, a few days after the final Allied saturation bombing of Berlin, the Soviets loosed their artillery against the overmatched German forces defending the Oder and the Neisse rivers, and eighteen Russian armies began to close their ring around the German capital, fifty miles to the west. Five days later, central Berlin came under direct artillery fire for the first time, and the city's 1.75 million remaining residents—mostly old men, women, and children—found themselves on the front line of a hopeless battle.

"It began with silence," wrote an anonymous Berliner of the final Soviet assault. "A far too silent night." Several hours later, the diarist awoke to the whistling of bullets and the rumbling of heavy guns. "The street is under fire. Men come stamping along: broad backs, leather jackets, high leather boots."

Berliners took refuge in underground shelters. According to the diarist, communities of citizens eked out an existence in "catacombs of fear, inhaling the noise of guns." Food was scarce. People depended on dwindling government rations and what they could scrounge from the cellars of abandoned buildings. They scuttled back and forth from the shelters, dodging artillery fire to collect water from standpipes in the streets. Russian soldiers helped themselves to the German women. Thousands of women of all ages were raped repeatedly, often while their husbands watched in horror.

At daybreak on May 2, Berlin's ragged defenders began to surrender—but not before Hitler's fanatical insistence that the capital be "defended to the last man and the last bullet" had ensured the needless sacrifice of thousands of civilians. The battle for Fortress Berlin had come to an end, but for months afterward, the people struggled to survive on little food and water, deprived of gas, electricity, telephones, or public transportation. In the end, the Berliners' resilient spirit prevailed. "I feel as though I've grown webs in order to swim through the mud," commented our diarist, "as though my fiber has become especially flexible and tough."

Berliners make their way through rubble-strewn streets following an Allied air raid in April 1945. A Soviet war correspondent who entered the city with the Red Army a few weeks later marveled at the Germans' resilience. "As soon as fighting stopped," he wrote, "people crept out of their holes and started life all over again."

Deciding To Leave or Stay

Frantic to flee Berlin, women and children crowd a railroad platform in early 1945. Their fear of the Russians was fueled by a government propaganda campaign detailing Soviet atrocities.

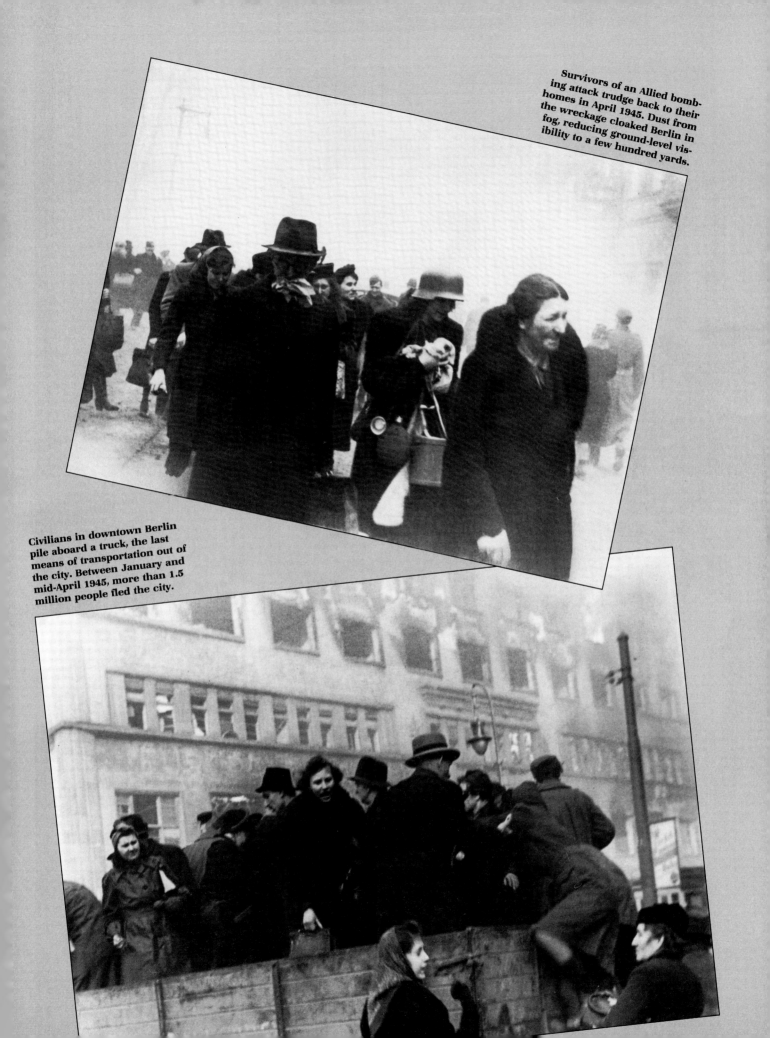

Survivors of an Allied bombing attack trudge back to their homes in April 1945. Dust from the wreckage cloaked Berlin in fog, reducing ground-level visibility to a few hundred yards.

Civilians in downtown Berlin pile aboard a truck, the last means of transportation out of the city. Between January and mid-April 1945, more than 1.5 million people fled the city.

Entrenched near a main street in Berlin, a teenaged member of the Hitler Youth and a middle-aged Volkssturm conscript nervously await the Russians. Each of them is equipped with a Panzerfaust antitank weapon that is capable of one shot.

Dead panzergrenadiers lie alongside an SS Wiking Division half-track. The critical shortage of arms and equipment in the spring of 1945 prompted a German general who inspected Berlin's defenses to pronounce them "utterly futile, ridiculous."

Belongings in tow, German families return to their wartorn neighborhoods following the Russian conquest. Whether they fled the city or remained behind, all Berliners shared the same fervent wish. "They want to live," reported the Soviet newspaper *Pravda*, "simply to live."

Seated in the dock at the Palace of Justice, the defendants *(left)* face the tribunal as prosecutor Robert H. Jackson, at the podium *(center)*, questions a witness *(top)*. Counsel for the defense, German lawyers chosen by the defendants from an approved list and paid for by the Americans, sit in front of the accused.

Justice at Nuremberg

Between November 1945 and October 1946, with the endorsement of the nineteen member states of the fledgling United Nations, the Allied powers brought to trial five Nazi organizations and twenty-two Nazi leaders. Never before had the principal figures of a defeated nation been prosecuted by a universally recognized court of law, and at first, a few voices questioned the legality of the proceedings. The voices of protest fell silent, however, as mountains of testimony revealed the incomparable crimes of Adolf Hitler's regime.

The German leaders faced a four-nation tribunal in Nuremberg, the city that had been the site of the annual party rallies during the Nazis' glory days. In a heavily guarded courtroom, the accused and their counsel heard the charges: planning and waging a war of aggression, violating the customs of war, and committing unprecedented "crimes against humanity." What defense could there be? As American prosecutor Robert H. Jackson stipulated, "one who committed criminal acts may not take refuge in superior orders nor in the doctrine that his crimes were acts of state."

It seemed like a dream, said armaments minister Albert Speer, to sit in a dank prison and see men once "expansive" in their magnificent uniforms now "shockingly run down" in black fatigues. Hans Frank, the governor-general of occupied Poland, converted to Catholicism a few weeks before the trial. General Alfred Jodl, OKW chief of operations, passed the hours refighting military campaigns. "Tell me frankly," Foreign Minister Joachim von Ribbentrop wrote to himself, "do any of us look like murderers?" With Hitler, Himmler, and Goebbels lost to suicide, leadership of the group fell to Hermann Göring, who was determined to maintain a united defense. But solidarity quickly frayed. Field Marshal Wilhelm Keitel was indignant at being tried with politicians. Banker Hjalmar Schacht called Göring an ignoramous. Anti-Semitic publisher and pornographer Julius Streicher was ostracized by all.

Day after day, the Allied prosecutors produced secret documents proving the defendants' complicity. When the court showed films of concentration-camp victims, propagandist Hans Fritzsche crumpled in his seat, slave labor czar Fritz Sauckel shuddered, and Reichsbank president Walther Funk wept. After 300,000 affidavits and a transcript of 10 million words, the trial had left its imprint. "A thousand years will pass," said Frank, "and still this guilt of Germany will not have been erased." Others were less moved. "In fifty or sixty years," Göring promised, "there will be statues of Hermann Göring all over Germany."

American guards keep an
around-the-clock vigil on the
defendants' six-by-twelve-foot
cells, whose only sources of light
were the lamps on the outside
wall. Wire mesh was put on the
upper level after a German general, awaiting trial on separate
charges, jumped to his death.

Days and Nights of Isolation

There were few creature comforts permitted the accused at Nuremberg. The prison guards poked them with poles if they slept facing the wall or put their hands under their blankets. After German Labor Front director Robert Ley hanged himself with a towel, chairs and all personal effects—even spectacles—were confiscated at night. The flimsy tables in the bare cells were designed to collapse if the defendants tried to stand on them.

The prisoners spent most of their days in solitary confinement and were forbidden to talk even during their daily thirty-minute walks in the exercise yard. Once the trial began, they were able to fraternize during lunch, served in several small rooms on an upper floor of the Palace of Justice. During the early months of the trial, Göring claimed his place at the head of the lunch table. To blunt the charismatic Reich marshal's influence, the jailers eventually separated the prisoners into six eating groups, with Göring dining alone.

Dressed in their courtroom clothes, Fritzsche, Schacht, and the diplomat-politician Franz von Papen *(left to right)* eat a meager meal. The prisoners' daily intake of calories was limited to 1,800.

Göring plots his defense with Otto Stahmer, a respected lawyer from Kiel. During five months of preparations, the Reich marshal lost sixty pounds and underwent withdrawal from an addiction to forty paracodeine pills a day.

Contrition
and Contempt
in the Dock

The defense strategies that were employed by Hermann Göring and Albert Speer could hardly have been more different. Identified as the "prime conspirator" by the tribunal, Göring stunned a world audience by taking the stand in his own defense and boasting vigorously of his role in the Nazis' rise to power. He took credit for creating the Sturmabteilung (SA), or Storm Troopers, reducing unemployment, rearming Germany, and assisting in the annexation of Austria. Details of the Nazi atrocities, he claimed, were not something he or the Führer was aware of. Fellow defendants were impressed with Göring's sharpness. "That is the Göring of the early days," Papen remarked.

Speer, in marked contrast, displayed a "more sincere and less demonstrative conception of the Nazi guilt than anyone else," according to the Vienna-born, American court psychologist, Captain Gustav M. Gilbert. Speer shocked his fellow defendants not only by admitting his effort to assassinate Hitler but also by fully acknowledging his role in exploiting the forced labor of foreigners in order to maintain the German war machine. He encouraged the German people to blame Hitler rather than the Allies for the destruction of their country. "Even in an authoritarian system, the leaders must accept a common responsibility," Speer announced, "and it is impossible for them to dodge that common responsibility after the catastrophe."

Albert Speer listens attentively to the trial proceedings. A British prosecutor called him "by far the most attractive personality among the defendants."

Göring glowers at the tribunal from his seat in the witness box. The Reich marshal took the stand amid widespread hope that he would be stripped of his haughty demeanor by the trial. Instead, he embarrassed the prosecution by correcting factual errors and criticizing the quality of the translations.

Rudolf Hess listens impassively as psychologist Gustav M. Gilbert *(hand on hip)* explains to counsel that amnesia prevents Hess from testifying on his own behalf. In other courtroom appearances, Hess appeared wracked with extreme mental anguish *(inset)*.

Pitiful Performances by Broken Men

None of the defendants gave more pathetic courtroom performances than Joachim von Ribbentrop, Hitler's foreign minister, and Rudolf Hess, one-time deputy führer who had been under British arrest since May 1941 when he astonished the world by flying alone to Scotland in an alleged attempt to make peace.

"My memory is again in order," Hess told the startled courtroom. But his claim to have feigned amnesia only helped to convince psychiatrists that he was mentally ill. For most of the proceedings, Hess complained that his food was being poisoned and he could not remember the date of his own birthday. During Rorschach inkblot tests, however, he recalled what he said were "bloody thoughts." After the court rejected a defense motion to dismiss charges against him on grounds of insanity, Hess sat woodenly through the rest of the trial, always bringing a book with him but never turning a page.

The formerly pompous Ribbentrop, in contrast, groveled before the court, sobbing and pleading his innocence. His emotional deterioration did not dim his admiration for the dead Führer, however. "If Hitler should come to me in my cell right now and say, 'Do this!' I would still do it," he confessed.

Stooped and pale, a distraught Joachim von Ribbentrop leans on the handrail. Ribbentrop spent much of the trial trying to justify the Reich's foreign policies, burying his anxiety, said Gilbert, "in a sea of memoranda and sleeping pills."

The official executioner, Master Sergeant John C. Woods, arrived at Nuremberg having hanged 347 men during a fifteen-year career. "I hanged those 10 Nazis," he later said, "and I am proud of it."

The Reckoning for Hitler's Henchmen

On September 30, 1946, the tribunal issued its verdicts. Sentenced to death by hanging were Göring, Ribbentrop, Streicher, Sauckel, Frank, Jodl, Keitel, Wilhelm Frick, minister of the interior, Ernst Kaltenbrunner, chief of the Reich Central Security Office, Alfred Rosenberg, party philosopher and Reich minister for the eastern occupied area, Artur Seyss-Inquart, Reich commissioner for the occupied Netherlands, and Martin Bormann *in absentia*. Hess and the supreme commander of the navy, Grand Admiral Erich Raeder, received life im-

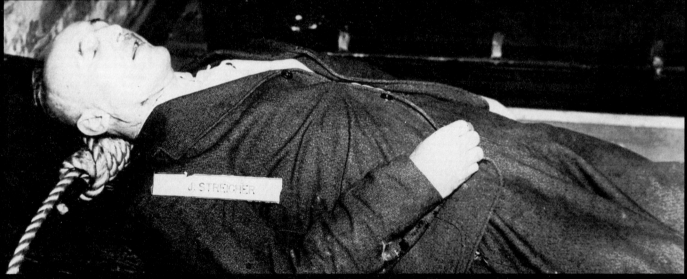

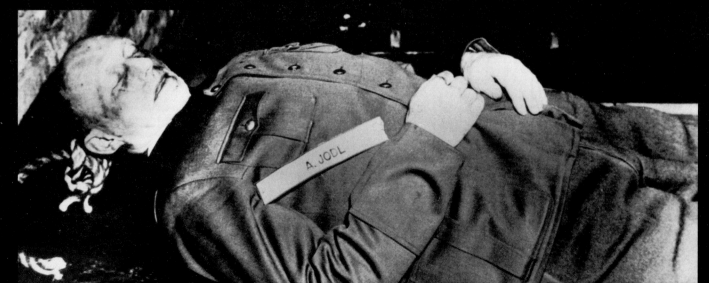

prisonment; Speer and Baldur von Schirach, head of the Hitler Youth, drew twenty-year prison terms; Constantin von Neurath, Reich protector of Bohemia and Moravia, fifteen years, and Grand Admiral Karl Dönitz, builder of the U-boat fleet and political successor to Hitler, ten years. Papen, Schacht, and Fritzsche were acquitted.

The hangings began in the predawn hours of October 16, 1945. Ribbentrop was the first of the convicted men to die. Jodl's indignant demand that he and Keitel face a traditional military firing squad was rejected by the tribunal. When Streicher mounted the gallows, he spat on the American hangman, telling him, "The Bolsheviks will hang you one day!" His last words were, "Heil Hitler!"

The bodies of the condemned Nazis were photographed for the record. Shown here are Streicher and Jodl *(opposite)*, Ribbentrop *(top)*, and Göring *(above)*, who swallowed a cyanide capsule two hours before his scheduled execution. How Göring got the capsule remains a mystery. Most likely, he received the poison from a bribed guard or had hidden it for months in his meerschaum pipe. By order of the court, Göring's ashes were thrown into the last functioning incinerator at Dachau.

BIBLIOGRAPHY

Books

Angolia, John R., *Edged Weaponry of the Third Reich*. Mountain View, Calif.: R. James Bender, 1974.

Bauer, Eddy, *Histoire Controversée de la Deuxième Guerre Mondiale, 1939-1945*. Monaco-Ville, Jaspard: Polus, 1966.

Beck, Earl R., *Under the Bombs: The German Home Front, 1942-1945*. Lexington: The University Press of Kentucky, 1986.

Bernage, Georges, *1944 Le Pont D'Arnhem*. Brussels: Editions J. M. Collet, 1980.

Blumenson, Martin, and the Editors of Time-Life Books, *Liberation* (World War II series). Alexandria, Va.: Time-Life Books, 1978.

Boldt, Gerhard, *Hitler's Last Days: An Eyewitness Account*. London: Sphere Books, 1973.

Bookman, John T., and Stephen T. Powers, *The March to Victory: A Guide to World War II Battles and Battlefields from London to the Rhine*. New York: Harper & Row, 1986.

Brett-Smith, Richard, *Hitler's Generals*. San Rafael, Calif.: Presidio Press, 1976.

Bridgman, Jon, *The End of the Holocaust: The Liberation of the Camps*. Ed. by Richard H. Jones. Portland, Oreg.: Areopagitica Press, 1990.

Bullock, Alan, *Hitler: A Study in Tyranny*. New York: Harper & Row, 1962.

Chamberlin, Brewster, and Marcia Feldman, eds., *The Liberation of the Nazi Concentration Camps, 1945: Eyewitness Accounts of the Liberators*. Washington, D.C.: United States Holocaust Memorial Council, 1987.

Cooper, Matthew, *The German Army, 1933-1945: Its Political and Military Failure*. London: MacDonald and Jane's, 1978.

Cowdery, Ray, *Hitler's New German Reichschancellery in Berlin, 1938-1945*. Küsnacht, Switzerland: Northstar Maschek, 1987.

Crookenden, Napier, *Battle of the Bulge, 1944*. New York: Charles Scribner's Sons, 1980.

Dollinger, Hans, *The Decline and Fall of Nazi Germany and Imperial Japan: A Pictorial History of the Last Days of World War II*. Transl. by Arnold Pomerans. New York: Crown, 1968.

Duffy, Christopher, *Red Storm on the Reich: The Soviet March on Germany, 1945*. New York: Atheneum, 1991.

Eisenberg, Azriel, *Witness to the Holocaust*. New York: The Pilgrim Press, 1981.

Erickson, John, *The Road to Berlin: Continuing the History of Stalin's War with Germany*. Boulder, Colo.: Westview Press, 1983.

Esposito, Vincent J., ed., *The West Point Atlas of American Wars, Vol. II, 1900-1953*. New York: Frederick A. Praeger, 1959.

Essame, H., *The Battle for Germany*. New York: Charles Scribner's Sons, 1969.

Fest, Joachim C., *Hitler*. Transl. by Richard and Clara Winston. New York: Random House, 1974.

Fey, Will, *Armor Battles of the Waffen-SS: 1943-45*. Transl. by Harri Henschler. Winnipeg, Manitoba: J. J. Fedorowicz, 1990.

Galante, Pierre, and Eugene Silianoff, *Voices from the Bunker*. Transl. by Jan Dalley. New York: G. P. Putnam's Sons, 1989.

Gilbert, Felix, *Hitler Directs His War*. New York: Oxford University Press, 1950.

Gilbert, Martin, *The Holocaust: A History of the Jews of Europe during the Second World War*. New York: Holt, Rinehart and Winston, 1985.

Goebbels, Joseph, *Final Entries, 1945: The Diaries of Joseph Goebbels*. Ed. by Hugh Trevor-Roper. New York: Avon, 1978.

Goolrick, William K., Ogden Tanner, and the Editors of Time-Life Books, *The Battle of the Bulge* (World War II series). Alexandria, Va.: Time-Life Books, 1979.

Grosrichard, Yves, *Histoire de la Guerre: 1939-1945*. Munich: Verlag Kurt Desch, 1965.

Guderian, Heinz, *Panzer Leader*. Transl. by Constantine FitzGibbon. Washington, D.C.: E. P. Dutton, 1952.

Heiber, Helmut, *Goebbels*. Transl. by John K. Dickinson. New York: Hawthorn Books, 1972.

Held, Werner, and Holger Nauroth, *The Defense of the Reich: Hitler's Nightfighter Planes and Pilots*. Transl. by David Roberts. New York: Arco, 1982.

Höhne, Heinz, *The Order of the Death's Head: The Story of Hitler's SS*. Transl. by Richard Barry. New York: Coward-McCann, 1969.

Irving, David, *The Destruction of Dresden*. New York: Holt, Rinehart and Winston, 1963.

Keegan, John, *The Second World War*. New York: Viking Press, 1990.

Kelley, Douglas M., *22 Cells in Nuremberg: A Psychiatrist Examines the Nazi Criminals*. New York: Greenberg, 1947.

Koch, H. W., *Hitler Youth: The Duped Generation*. New York: Ballantine Books, 1972.

Kuby, Erich, *The Russians and Berlin, 1945*. Transl. by Arnold J. Pomerans. London: Heinemann, 1965.

Lang, Jochen von, *The Secretary: Martin Bormann, the Man Who Manipulated Hitler*. Transl. by Christa Armstrong and Peter White. New York: Random House, 1979.

Lehndorff, Hans Graf von, *Token of a Covenant: Diary of an East Prussian Surgeon, 1945-1947*. Transl. by Elizabeth Mayer. Chicago: Henry Regnery, 1964.

Le Tissier, Tony, *The Battle of Berlin, 1945*. New York: St. Martin's Press, 1988.

Liddell Hart, B. H.:
History of the Second World War. New York: G. P. Putnam's Sons, 1971.
The Other Side of the Hill: Germany's Generals, Their Rise and Fall, with Their Own Account of Military Events, 1939-1945. London: Cassell, 1948.

Livingston, Jane, *Lee Miller: Photographer*. New York: Thames and Hudson, 1989.

Lucas, James, *Last Days of the Third Reich: The Collapse of Nazi Germany, May 1945*. New York: William Morrow, 1986.

Luck, Hans von, *Panzer Commander: The Memoirs of Colonel Hans von Luck*. New York: Praeger, 1989.

MacDonald, Charles B., *The Siegfried Line Campaign*. Washington, D.C.: Office of the Chief of Military History, United States Army, 1963.

Madeja, W. Victor, *The Russo-German War: 25 January to 8 May, 1945*. Allentown, Pa.: Valor, 1987.

Maier, Georg, *Drama Zwischen Budapest und Wien: Der Endkampf der 6. Panzerarmee 1945*. Osnabrück: Munin-Verlag, 1985.

Mellenthin, Friedrich W. von, *German Generals of World War II: As I Saw Them*. Norman: University of Oklahoma Press, 1977.

Mitcham, Samuel W., Jr., *Hitler's Legions: The German Army Order of Battle, World War II*. New York: Dorset Press, 1985.

Mosley, Leonard O.:
The Reich Marshal: A Biography of Hermann Goering. Garden City, N.Y.: Doubleday, 1974.
Report from Germany. London: Victor Gollancz, 1945.

O'Donnell, James P., *The Bunker: The History of the Reich Chancellery Group*. New York: Bantam Books, 1978.

Pallud, Jean-Paul, *Ardennes 1944: Peiper and Skorzeny*. London: Osprey, 1987.

Piekalkiewicz, Janusz, *Arnhem 1944*. Transl. by H. A. and A. J. Barker. New York: Charles Scribner's Sons, 1976.

Reimann, Viktor, *Goebbels*. Transl. by Stephen Wendt. Garden City, N.Y.: Doubleday, 1976.

Reitlinger, Gerald, *The SS: Alibi of a Nation, 1922-1945*. London: Arms and Armour Press, 1981.

Riess, Curt, *Joseph Goebbels*. London: Hollis and Carter, 1949.

Ryan, Cornelius, *A Bridge Too Far*. New York: Simon and Schuster, 1974.

Salmaggi, Cesare, and Alfredo Pallavisini, comps., *2194 Days of War*. New York: Gallery Books, 1979.

Scheibert, Horst, *Panzer Grenadier Division Grossdeutschland: A Pictorial History with Text & Maps*. Ed. by Bruce Culver, transl. by Gisele Hockenberry. Warren, Mich.: Squadron/Signal, 1977.

Seaton, Albert:
The Fall of Fortress Europe, 1943-1945. New York: Holmes & Meier, 1981.
The German Army, 1933-45. New York: St. Martin's Press, 1982.
The Russo-German War. New York: Praeger, 1971.

Semmler, Rudolf, *Goebbels: The Man Next to Hitler*. London: Westhouse, 1947.

Speer, Albert, *Inside the Third Reich*. Ed. by Richard and Clara Winston. New York: Macmillan, 1970.

Steinert, Marlis G.:
Hitler's War and the Germans: Public Mood and Attitude during the Second World War. Athens: Ohio University Press, 1977.
23 Days: The Final Collapse of Nazi Germany. Transl. by Richard Barry. New York: Walker, 1969.

Storia Della Seconda Guerra Mondiale (Vol. 6). Milan, Italy: Rizzoli Editore, 1967.

Strawson, John, *Hitler's Battles for Europe*. New York: Charles Scribner's Sons, 1971.

Thorwald, Juergen, *Flight in the Winter*. Ed. and transl. by Fred Wieck. New York: Pantheon, 1951.

Trevor-Roper, Hugh R., *The Last Days of Hitler*. New York: Macmillan, 1947.

Walther, Herbert, *Die 12. SS-Panzer-Division HJ*. Darmstadt, Germany: Podzun-Pallas-Verlag, 1987.

Warlimont, Walter, *Inside Hitler's Headquarters, 1939-45*. Transl. by R. H. Barry, New York: Frederick A. Praeger, 1964.

Whiting, Charles:
'45: The Final Drive from the Rhine to the Baltic. London: Century, 1985.
Skorzeny. New York: Ballantine Books, 1972.

Whiting, Charles, and the Editors of Time-Life Books, *The Home Front: Germany* (World War II series). Alexandria, Va.: 1982.

Wilmot, Chester, *The Struggle for Europe*. New York: Harper & Brothers, 1952.

Ziemke, Earl F.:
Stalingrad to Berlin: The German Defeat in the East. Washington, D.C.: Office of the Chief of Military History, United States Army, 1968.
The U.S. Army in the Occupation of Germany: 1944-1946. Washington, D.C.: Center of Military History, United States Army, 1975.

Other Publications

"Battle for Aachen." *After the Battle*, no. 42.

"The Battle of Arnhem." *After the Battle*, no. 2.

"Battle of the Bulge." *After the Battle*, no. 4.

Pallud, Jean-Paul, "Battle of the Bulge: Then and Now." *After the Battle*, no. 40.

U.S. Seventh Army, "Dachau." Comp. by William W. Quinn. n.p., n.d.

Acknowledgments

The editors thank the following individuals: Austria: Vienna—Manfred Rauchensteiner, Heeresgeschichtliches Museum. Canada: Peter C. Hoffmann, Westmount. Germany: Berlin—Wilfried Gopel, Archiv für Kunst und Geschichte; Heidi Klein, Bildarchiv Preussischer Kulturbesitz; Wolfgang Streubel, Ullstein Bilderdienst. Koblenz—Meinrad Nilges, Bundesarchiv. Munich—Elisabeth Heidt, Süddeutscher Verlag Bilderdienst; Robert Hoffmann, Presseillustrationen Heinrich R. Hoffmann. Osnabrück—Karl-Walter Becker. Rösrath-Hoffnungsthal—Helga Müller, Archiv Piekalkiewicz. Stuttgart—Angelika Treiber, Bibliothek für Zeitgeschichte. United States: Delaware—Richard Raiber, Hockessin. District of Columbia—Stig Forster, German Historical Institute. Virginia—Paul J. Gartenmann, Falls Church. Washington—Jon M. Bridgman, University of Washington.

Picture Credits

Credits from left to right are separated by semicolons; from top to bottom by dashes.

Cover: Johnny Florea for LIFE. 4, 5: Presseillustrationen Heinrich R. Hoffmann, Munich. 6: S.I.R.P.A./E.C.P. Armées, Paris. 9: Map by R. R. Donnelley & Sons Company, Cartographic Services. 13: Imperial War Museum, London. 15: Hans Kramp, Linnich. 16: Ullstein Bilderdienst, Berlin. 18: Bundesarchiv, Koblenz. 19: Bildarchiv J. K. Piekalkiewicz, Rösrath-Hoffnungsthal. 21: Bundesarchiv, Koblenz. 22, 23: Imperial War Museum, London. 25: Ullstein Bilderdienst, Berlin. 26: Süddeutscher Verlag Bilderdienst, Munich. 27: UPI/Bettmann, New York— Süddeutscher Verlag Bilderdienst, Munich. 28-31: From *Der Zweite Weltkreig im Bild*/Burda, Verlag Offenburg, 1952. 33: Ullstein Bilderdienst, Berlin. 34, 35: UPI/Bettmann, New York. 38, 39: National Archives 111-SC-198252. 40, 41: From *Ardennes 1944: Peiper and Skorzeny* by Jean-Paul Pallud, Osprey Publishing, London, 1987; Dutch State Institute for War Documentation, Amsterdam—Jean-Paul Pallud. 44, 45: Jean-Paul Pallud. 47: Map by R. R. Donnelley & Sons Company, Cartographic Services. 48, 49: AP/Wide World, New York, inset Bildarchiv Preussischer Kulturbesitz, Berlin. 50, 51: Bundesarchiv, Koblenz. 52, 53: Presseillustrationen Heinrich R. Hoffmann, Munich; UPI/Bettmann, New York—Bundesarchiv, Koblenz. 54, 55: S.I.R.P.A./E.C.P. Armées, Paris; Bildarchiv Preussischer Kulturbesitz, Berlin, Foto, Benno Wundshammer. 56: Bildarchiv Preussischer Kulturbesitz, Berlin. 59: Presseillustrationen Heinrich R. Hoffmann, Munich. 60, 61: Map by R. R. Donnelley & Sons Company, Cartographic Services. 63, 67: Bildarchiv Preussischer Kulturbesitz, Berlin. 68, 69: Ullstein Bilderdienst, Berlin. 71: Archiv Gerstenberg, Wietze. 72: Ullstein Bilderdienst, Berlin. 74, 76: Süddeutscher Verlag Bilderdienst, Munich. 79: From *Das Ende an der Elbe* by Jurgen Thorwald, Im Bertelamann Lesring, 1959, courtesy Bibliothek für Zeitgeschichte, Stuttgart. 81: Foto Werner Schüring, from *So fiel Königsberg* by General Otto Lasch, Gräfe und Unzer Verlag, Munich, no date— Keystone, Paris. 83-85: Helmuth Spaeter, Eching-Ammersee. 86, 87: From *Die Letzten Hundert Tage* by Dr. Hans-Adolf Jacobsen, Wiesbaden, 1965; Ullstein Bilderdienst, Berlin. 88: Carl Henrich, Traben-Trarbach. 91: Map by R. R. Donnelley & Sons Company, Cartographic Services. 92, 93: From *Histoire Controversée de la Deuxième Guerre Mondiale, 1939-1945* by Eddy Bauer, Monaco-Ville, Jaspard, Polus, 1967/DR. 95: Süddeutscher Verlag Bilderdienst, Munich. 96: Ullstein Bilderdienst, Berlin. 98, 99: Ullstein Bilderdienst, Berlin, inset map by R. R. Donnelley & Sons Company, Cartographic Services. 100-103: Ullstein Bilderdienst, Berlin. 104, 105: Bundesarchiv, Koblenz, inset from *Die 1.SS-Panzer-Division, Leibstandarte* by Herbert Walther, Podzun-Pallas-Verlag, Friedberg, 1987. 106, 107: Militärhistorischer Dienst, Bundesministerium für Landerverteidigung, inset from *Die Leibstandarte Im Bild* by Rudolf Lehmann, Munin-Verlag, Osnabrück, 1983. 108, 109: Süddeutscher Verlag Bilderdienst, Berlin. 110, 111: AP/Wide World, New York; Yad Vashem, Jerusalem. 112, 113: © 1985 Lee Miller Archives, Chiddingly, East Sussex; British Information Services, New York. 114, 115: Photoreporters, New York; AP/Wide World, New York. 116: Süddeutscher Verlag Bilderdienst, Munich. 119, 121: Presseillustrationen Heinrich R. Hoffmann, Munich. 122: UPI/Bettmann, New York. 123: Heinrich R. Hoffmann. 126: Süddeutscher Verlag Bilderdienst, Munich. 127: Süddeutscher Verlag Bilderdienst, Munich. 129: Presseillustrationen Heinrich R. Hoffmann, Munich. 131: Süddeutscher Verlag Bilderdienst, Munich (3), bottom from *Hitler's Personal Security* by Peter Hoffmann, M.I.T. Press, 1979. 133: Ullstein Bilderdienst, Berlin. 135: Bildarchiv Preussischer Kulturbesitz, Berlin. 136: Bildarchiv Preussischer Kulturbesitz, Berlin. 137: Archives Tallandier, Paris. 138, 139: Ullstein Bilderdienst, Berlin. 140: Courtesy Albert Sherman. 141: Bildarchiv Preussischer Kulturbesitz, Berlin. 143: Süddeutscher Verlag Bilderdienst, Munich; Ullstein Bilderdienst, Berlin. 144, 145: From *The Defense of the Reich*, translated by David Roberts, Arco Publishing, New York, 1982. 146, 147: Presseillustrationen Heinrich R. Hoffmann, Munich. 149: Presseillustrationen Heinrich R. Hoffmann, Munich— Süddeutscher Verlag Bilderdienst, Munich. 150, 151: Ullstein Bilderdienst, Berlin. 152: Photo by Michael Freeman, courtesy private collection—Bildarchiv Preussischer Kulturbesitz, Berlin. 155: Bildarchiv Preussischer Kulturbesitz, Berlin. 157: Ullstein Bilderdienst, Berlin. 158, 159: Süddeutscher Verlag Bilderdienst, Munich. 160: Bildarchiv Preussischer Kulturbesitz, Berlin. 161: Ullstein Bilderdienst, Berlin— Photoreporters, New York. 162, 163: Ullstein Bilderdienst, Berlin; Bildarchiv Preussischer Kulturbesitz, Berlin. 164, 165: Fotokhronika Tass, Moscow. 166, 167: Courtesy Time Inc. Magazines Picture Collection. 168: National Archives 11-SC-218565. 169: Roger-Viollet, Paris—Yergeni Khaldei, Moscow. 170: National Archives 11-SC-252940. 171: Yergeni Khaldei, Moscow. 172: Süddeutscher Verlag Bilderdienst, Munich—Roger-Viollet, Paris. 173: National Archives 111-SC-218562. 174: Süddeutscher Verlag Bilderdienst, Munich—The Bettmann Archive, New York—Ullstein Bilderdienst, Berlin. 175: The Bettmann Archive, New York—UPI/Bettmann, New York.

Index

Numerals in italics indicate an illustration of the subject mentioned.

A

Aachen: 11, 14, 31, 32, 33, 35, 37; Allied capture of, 21-24, *25-27*, 47
Aachen Gap: 22
Abwehr: 119
Adlerhorst: Hitler's western front headquarters at, *57, 58, 60,* 65
Aircraft: Arado 96 trainer, 144; Fieseler Storch reconnaissance plane, 142; Focke Wulf 190, 141; Ju-52 transports, 42; Ju-87 dive bombers (Stukas), 70; Ju-88 transports, 42; Lancaster bombers (British), 28; Messerschmitt 262 jet fighters, 124; Typhoon bombers (British), 30
Albert Canal: 12, 13, 14
Allies: agreement with Soviets over transfer of POWs, 83; air support for ground troops, 21, 32, 42, 46, 144; attacks on evacuation ships in Baltic, 73; Baltic port cities as objective of, 86, 96, 97; bombing of German cities by, 20, 95, 96, 97, 117, 125, 130-132, 135, *136-137,* 157, 158, 161; breakout from Normandy beachheads, 9, 118; demand for German unconditional surrender, 125; German hopes for dissension among, 8, 39, 69, 138, 143; and Nuremberg tribunal, 155, 156, 167; offensive capability of German army in the west underestimated by, 35, 39, 40; replacement of Soviet army equipment, 100; strategic plans of, 11-12, 14-15, 22, 97, 125; supply problems of, 11, 12, 14, 23, 24, 30-31
Alpine Redoubt: 97, 125, 138-139
Alsace: 10, 11, 35
Antwerp: 9, 11, 12, 24, 29, 30-31, 33, 36, 37, 40, 43, 47; German POWs in, *13*
Ardennes Forest: German offensive in, *6, 34-37, 38-39, 40, 41, 42-43, 44-45,* 46, *map* 47, 57, 90, 99
Armed forces high command (OKW): 7, 10, 13, 22, 35, 36, 37, 38, 39, 43
Armed Forces Netherlands: 17, 18, 35
Armored vehicles: Churchill tanks (Allied), 100; Cromwell tanks (Allied), 100; half-tracks, *6, 98-99, 162-163;* Panther tanks, *44, 102-103;* personnel carriers, *81, 86-87;* Royal Tiger tanks, 42; self-propelled assault guns (Soviet), *71;* Sherman tanks (Allied), *27, 100; Sturmgeschütz* III assault guns, *26, 68-69*
Army: casualties, 10, 20, 32, 46, 65, 80, 82, 83, 88, 91, 95, 97; command operations for Ardennes offensive, 35; disintegration of, 65, 91, 104, 154; horse transport for, *63;* Nazi political officers in, 126-128; panzergrenadiers, *38-39,* 82, *86-87, 98-99, 162-163;* reconnaissance team, *100-101;* recovery of on western front, 14, 20, 33-34; and Reserve Army, 12, 120; snow

camouflage uniforms, *68-69;* summary executions in, *76,* 77-78, 89, 94; underage recruits for, *cover;* volksgrenadier divisions, 12, 20, 26, 37, 42, 120; women auxiliaries in, 123. *See also* Volkssturm
Army (armored units): Second Panzer Army, 77; Third Panzer Army, 60, 62, 67, 77, *86-87,* 88; Fourth Panzer Army, 58, 60, 62; Fifth Panzer Army, 10, 14, 20-21, 32, 35, 36, 43, 44, 47; I Panzer Corps, 42; XXIV Panzer Corps, 62; XLVII Panzer Corps, 43; LVI Panzer Corps, 78; LXVIII Panzer Corps, 62; Panzer Corps Grossdeutschland, 63; 2d Panzer Division, 43; 7th Panzer Division, 63; 21st Panzer Division, 66; 116th Panzer Division, *6;* Grossdeutschland Panzergrenadier Division, 63; Panzer Lehr Division, 43; 125th Regiment, 66, 70
Army (infantry units): First Army, 94; First Paratroop Army, 12-13, 17, 20, 35, 93; Second Army, 60, 64, 67, 70; Third Army, 70; Fourth Army, 60, 66, 67, 81; Sixth Army, 105; Seventh Army, 10, 22, 32, 36, 43; Ninth Army, 8, 58, 62, 67, 70, 79, 88, 89; Twelfth Army, 90, 144, 146; Fifteenth Army, 10, 12, 15, 17, 24, 35; Seventeenth Army, 58, 62, 67; XLII Corps, 62; LVII Corps, 145; LXXXI Corps, 22; 12th Infantry Division, 22; 26th Volksgrenadier Division, 43; 49th Infantry Division, 22; 59th Infantry Division, 17; 64th Infantry Division, 24, 28; 70th Infantry Division, 24, 30; 183d Volksgrenadier Division, 22; 245th Infantry Division, 24, 30; 246th Volksgrenadier Division, 22, 25; Grossdeutschland Division, *83-85;* 6th Paratroop Regiment, 28; Hermann Göring Replacement Training Regiment, 28; Task Force Chill, 28; Task Force Walther, 19
Army Detachment Samland: 70
Army Group A: 58, 60, 61, 63, 65, 69
Army Group B: 10, 12, 13, 14, 32, 35, 90, 91, 96
Army Group Center: 9, 48, 60, 61, 63, 64, 66, 69, 70, 76, 77, 89
Army Group Courland: 82
Army Group G: 8-10, 12, 13, 14, 20, 35, 91
Army Group H: 35
Army Group North: 57, 61, 65, 69
Army Group South: 58, 61, 77
Army Group Vistula: 67, 69, 75, 76, 78, 79, 82, 88, 89, 128
Army high command (OKH): 57, 58, 60, 65, 75, 89
Arnhem: 15, 20, 21, 33, 47; Allied airdrop at, *16,* 18
Arnswalde: 76
Artillery: coastal batteries, *28,* 30; 88-mm guns, 18; mobile rocket launchers (American), *33;* 155-mm guns, 24, *25;* rocket launchers (Soviet), 80
Atlantic Wall: 10, 24
Atomic bomb: German scientific research

for, 124
Auschwitz concentration camp: Soviet liberation of, 67
Austria: and Alpine Redoubt, 97, 125; German forces in, 88, 154; Soviet advances in, 61, 106
Awards: Iron Cross, 143; Iron Cross, Second Class, 95; Knight's Cross of the Iron Cross, diamond clasp for, 8; shortages of, 44

B

Baden-Württemberg: 134
Balck, Hermann: 20, 105
Balkans: German forces in, 57, 69, 154
Baltic Sea: German evacuations, 72; ports as Allied objectives, 86, 96
Baranow: 58, 60, 61
Bastogne: 43-44
Battle of the Bulge: 43. *See also* Ardennes
Baur, Hans: *4-5,* 150
Bavaria: and Alpine Redoubt, 97, 125
Beermann, Helmut: 139
Belgium: Allied advances in, 9, 11, 12; Ardennes offensive, 34-47; German defensive positions in, 10, 13; German scorched earth policy in, 132
Benz, Siegfried: *126-127*
Berchtesgaden: 118, 138, 140, 153
Bergen-Belsen concentration camp: Allied liberation of, 108, 110, 114; burials at, *113*
Berghof: 140
Berlin: 78, 97, 117, 125, 138, 141; attempts to lift Soviet siege, 144, 146, 148; civilian evacuation of, *160, 161;* civilian ordeal during battle for, 144-145, *157-165;* feeble defensive resources at, 88, 118, 145, *162-163;* German surrender in, *152-153,* 154; Hitler moves headquarters to, 65; Hitler's determination to defend, 126, 139, 144; return of peace to, *164-165;* as Soviet objective, 46, 58, 61, 67, 76, 77, 79, 82, 86, 89-90, 97
Bernadotte, Count Folke: 142, 143, 156
Bernau: 90
Best, Werner: 124
Blaskowitz, Johannes: 8, 12, 14, 20
Boldt, Gerhard: 146
Bonn: 94
Bormann, Martin: 48, 64, 73-74, 125, 133, 134, 150-151; escape from Führer Bunker and death of, 152-153; at the Führer Bunker, 140, 147, 148; growing power of, 119, 126-129; and Hitler, 117, *129,* 139; and Nuremberg tribunal, 174
Bradley, Omar N.: 11, 31, 32, 40, 97
Brandenberger, Erich: 22, 36
Brandenburg: 70, 76
Braun, Eva: 128, 139, *146,* 151, 152; marriage certificate of, *147;* marries Hitler in underground bunker, 147-148; suicide of, 150
Braun, Gretl: 146
Bremen: 156